1.⁰⁰
p

The
MEAT BOARD MEAT BOOK

by Barbara Bloch

With an Introduction by
Julia Child

A BENJAMIN COMPANY BOOK

McGraw-Hill Book Company

New York   St. Louis   San Francisco
London   Düsseldorf   Mexico   Panama
Toronto   Sydney

Special thanks to my husband Ted Benjamin, who manages to make his perceptive critiques of both my writing and cooking sound like compliments, and whose "blue pencil" is unerringly accurate.

Thanks also to that meat cutter extraordinaire, Paul Belcastro, who found time to answer my endless questions.

To have both a loving husband and a good butcher is to be twice blessed!

B.B.

Copyright © 1977 by National Live Stock & Meat Board and The Benjamin Company, Inc.

Library of Congress Catalog Card Number: 76-52873
ISBN: Hardcover 0-07-005908-X; Paperback 0-07-005909-8

Published with the National Live Stock & Meat Board, Chicago, by The Benjamin Company, Inc., 485 Madison Avenue, New York, N.Y. 10022.

Distributed by McGraw-Hill Book Company
Art Director: Winston Potter
First printing: July, 1977

The Meat Board Meat Book

Contents

Introduction by Julia Child

The Meat Board has done it again! Not only have they come up with a standardized nomenclature system for all meat cuts, but now the Board has developed this most useful and informative handbook for all of us to have and to hold, and to learn from. Learning about meat means knowing how to shop for meat, and to care for it when you bring it home, and then, of course, knowing how to cook it. Meat purchases make up the largest part of the family food budget. Since meat is also our most nourishing food, it behooves us all to be as meat-wise as possible.

The meat-wise state of knowledge, however, is not bred into us; we have to work at it. This means taking meat seriously and making a challenging hobby of it, for a while at least. To make it more of a challenge, and also more fun, you might make a family game of it. Your children will bless you later for their early initiation. When you go to market, for example, take this book and the family with you, and together start studying various cuts of meat. You might spend 10 minutes at the meat counter, picking out and comparing various cuts of beef chuck, memorizing and discussing their bone structures, their shapes, and their identifying features. The next time you market, see how well you have remembered your first lesson. Then move to other parts of the animal and to other animals. Just the fact of studying and discussing will fix meat cuts in your mind's eye and gradually you will find that you really know your meat.

At home, using a reliable book of directions, try out the various basic cooking methods. If you can do it together, as a family, all the better. One day do a boiled dinner, another day a pot roast, then a stew with vegetables. That's the way to learn: start right in cooking, always keeping notes on what you do and how it turns out. You will thus develop your own personal style, as well as confidence in yourself as a cook. Take lessons, too, if any are available, and cook with knowledgeable friends, because one of the best ways to learn anything is to work right beside an expert.

7

Even an expert, though, will rarely have in hand or head all the information offered to you in this book. Not only does it give you an illustrated and descriptive guide to identifying the actual pieces of meat you will encounter at your market, but you will know about grades of meat, the aging of meat, plus how much to buy and how best to cook it. Then, if the carver in the family has always dreaded slicing a roast shoulder of pork at the table before family and friends, or has the jitters when standing, knife poised, over a leg of lamb or a brisket, get a good knife, following the advice here. Sharpen it as illustrated, and the carving directions will show the way.

Are you tempted to buy a whole beef carcass or side of lamb, and butcher it yourself? Better read about the costs and pitfalls before you spend your money. What is the best way to keep your meat, and what about freezing and freezers? Are your barbecues a disaster? Find out the answers to those questions in these pages. Do you need a new stove? What about microwave ovens? Be a tough customer, this book advises, and then goes on to tell you how not to be fooled by labels and advertising, and other gimmickry. How refreshing it is to read some frank talk when we are so much surrounded by the bland goody goody language of our daily publicists.

Thus I am delighted to introduce you to the *Meat Board Meat Book*. Take it to bed with you and study the charts. Have it handy in the kitchen to consult with or to accompany you when you shop. And remember, the more you work on learning your trade as a meat cook, the better and more economical a shopper you will be, and the more pleasure you and your whole family will have when you cook and dine together.

Bon appetit!
Julia Child

Foreword

There is probably more irritation, frustration, and confusion per square inch at the immaculate, chilled, long, white, sterile meat counter in a modern supermarket than almost anywhere else in a homemaker's shopping routine.

On the consumer's side of the counter, that is.

Over on the friendly butcher's side there are product knowledge, flashing blades, nomenclature, and clickety-clackety machines that weigh, package, label, and price with flawless automatic precision.

On the consumer's side there may be full and complete knowledge of Porterhouse steaks, rump roasts, pork loin chops, bacon, ham, lamb patties, wieners, and mounds of ground beef. But what the average consumer does not know about the other 306 meat cuts (about one-third of which are apt to be available at any given time) could fill a book.

As a matter of fact, that's what we've done . . . fill a book. This book, *The Meat Board Meat Book*. We've been in the business of helping consumers for more than fifty years and we've finally gotten around to preparing a major book for people who shop for and prepare meat. To add zest to the book and to expand slightly beyond the basics that every meat shopper ought to have comfortably in mind, author Barbara Bloch has even added a detailed glossary—plus a special one on restaurant terminology in five languages!

Speaking of Barbara, she's intrepid. She argued over this book with the *creme de la creme* of meat experts (that's us) for twelve months. Experts we are, undeniably. But occasionally we've been stuffy about our subject, reluctant sometimes to admit that once in a while there's a piece of second-rate meat served at a first-rate price, or even (may their numbers decrease) a storekeeper with a thumb on the scale, or anyone so grossly inadequate as to expect good results from using a "wrong" cooking method.

Anyway, Barbara now knows even more about meat than she did when she undertook this project. And we know more about our customers. If we are correct about this Bloch-Meat

Board adventure, every reader will be the beneficiary. But we also believe that our industry will benefit because a well-informed consumer is a repeat customer. And that's what we want, satisfied customers coming back again and again, served by consistent performance at the meat counter.

The National Live Stock & Meat Board had been in business for more than half a century when the idea for this practical consumer book was germinated several years ago.

The Meat Board is a unique organization, unlike any other in the food industry. It develops information and facts about meat and provides special services for consumers or consumer interests (including medical, public health, government groups, food editors and writers, retailers, and other food industry organizations). It is also the major promotion agency for the farmers and processors of the beef, pork, and lamb industry.

We have earnestly sought solutions to consumer frustrations at both the meat counter and in the kitchen since 1922. But there are always new shoppers coming of age, and old problems have a way of repeating themselves and becoming new ones for the inexperienced homemaker. And technology creates new problems. So does genetic improvement, as farmers try to breed ever more efficient cattle, hogs, and sheep.

Many frustrations have been resolved over the years by our activities in the fields of home economics, experimentation with cooking methods, recipe development, equipment testing, meat-cutting instruction for retailers, and in nutrition research—all intended to help consumers become better informed, more careful, value-conscious shoppers.

But, of course, some problems have not been solved. Just ask veteran meat shoppers what they think about prepackaged, self-service meat displays. They may acknowledge that self-service has lowered costs, increased efficiency, and probably improved sanitation. But they'll also tell you it has removed personal contact with the butcher, an important source of information on meal planning. As a result, there is a vacuum in the area of customer confidence.

Self-service has also somewhat limited the butcher's handling of meat and his personal knowledge of, and identification with, the cuts in his counter. In addition, he has lost contact with his customers. It has removed him from his traditional sales and public relations job.

Well, lamenting all that lost contact—except at those rare, fully staffed meat counters where contact still exists—

doesn't solve the frustrations. So with these thoughts in mind, I asked my wife what she did when a cut of meat didn't live up to its implied promise.

"I go back and hit the butcher over the head with the bone," she replied, with inelegant emphasis.

On that day was born a determination to redouble Meat Board efforts to improve instructions to American meat shoppers (to save them from the necessity of an angry return to the meat counter). We knew, too, we'd have to provide more assistance to the meat cutter behind the counter, not only to save him a dented head, but also to help him build loyalty and keep his customers.

Here we were, the nation's experts on fresh meat, with a half century's experience and lore about beef, pork, lamb, and veal (nobody, but nobody, knows more about meat than our collective staff of home economists, meat and animal scientists, nutrition-science experts, and marketing specialists), yet the wife of the chief executive was threatening butchers with ham bones and the like!

Our chartered mission is to help consumers be effective meat shoppers and cooks and to help the industry increase its understanding of consumers while improving its products. In keeping with that mission, we began to develop two major projects. One was to be this book, *The Meat Board Meat Book*. (Well, what would you call it?)

The other undertaking involved nomenclature. Even before the book could be written, there had to be a minor revolution in that phase of the distribution end of our farm-to-market chain. There were just too many names for the various cuts of meat. After checking with a number of meat retailers who agreed to support the project, we began the development of a long-overdue national uniform system of positive meat identification standards for consumers. This system would be basic to any "all about" discussion of meat, which the book (this book) was to be.

The system had to be simple enough to be understood by new and inexperienced young shoppers.

The system had to be universal in its design so that most, if not all, of the 220,000 retailers who sell meat could adapt it to their own merchandising schemes.

The system had to guarantee to consumers that wherever they might shop for meat, in any part of the United States, the same meat cut would be labeled with the same name.

The system had to bring about the demise of such vague names as "His 'n' Hers Steaks," or such glamorous handles as

"Paradise Roast"—the end, that is, of fanciful, alluring, non-descriptive, perhaps even deceptive, names on meat cuts.

The system had to reduce the names of meat cuts to sensible numbers. The program trimmed meat names from a formidable list of more than 1,000 to just 314—one official name for each different cut of beef, pork, lamb, and veal.

It took more than two years to develop what is now known as the Uniform Retail Meat Identity Standards program, mercifully abbreviated to URMIS. Independent and chain grocers, retail butchers, and meat packers from across the country were consulted. Many retail leaders were so pleased with the concept of uniform identity standards that they offered extra assistance. Local, state, and federal regulators who were concerned with advertising, packaging, and weights and measures were helpful. We also sought opinions from organized consumer activist groups. (One meat-boycott leader from California—circa 1973-74—when asked what she thought of it, praised the program with, "It's about damned time!")

After the URMIS program was introduced to the trade and the public (and immediately accepted by consumers) we started the serious outline for this basic meat book. Research determined which of the 314 "official" meat cuts were most commonly seen in meat counters. Then months of photography were followed by another year of planning and execution of the book. Barbara Bloch, cooking instructor, food writer, and long-time meat shopper, took on the writing assignment and began by interviewing a dozen or so meat-science, home-economics, and nutrition experts on our staff.

Julia Child, that remarkable American chef, thought the book a grand idea and agreed to write an introduction. On her television program, *The French Chef*, and in her newspaper and magazine columns, she had long touted one of our college food-science textbooks, *Lessons on Meat*, as a basic primer to understanding meat preparation and cooking. And she wrote the very first nonindustry book using the URMIS identification system, including applicable portions of it in her marvelous 1975 cookbook, *From Julia Child's Kitchen*.

But though we encouraged Julia to "scoop" us, it is here in *The Meat Board Meat Book* that the first full-color presentation of the new American identity standards appears in print. The standards are invaluable to shoppers. They are applauded by consumer activists. They are easily adapted by the retail industry. They are approved by the United States Department of Agriculture, the White House Office for Consumer Affairs, the Federal Trade Commission, and by the offices of attorneys-general or consumer affairs—or both—in thirty-five states and several municipalities.

Speaking of the extraordinary and singular Julia Child, I had envisioned this book to be one that she herself would either have ordered or written if ever she'd had the time. She is joined by other talented American chefs and food writers who agree that a basic understanding of food must precede any attempts at cooking, whether basic meals or nonbasic gourmet fare.

And *The Meat Board Meat Book* is just that. It is basic. It is a kind of popular, zestier version of our long-respected textbook, *Lessons on Meat*. True, homemakers have found, as did Julia Child, that *Lessons on Meat* is a handy manual. But it was written and intended for use in a home economics classroom under a teacher's instruction.

This book, on the other hand, should make good arm chair reading or interesting casual scanning at the kitchen table. It is a ready kitchen reference. Its identification, carving, buying, storage, preparation, cooking method, and serving sections complement every homemaker's cookbook collection, from *Mastering the Art of French Cooking* to recipes clipped from newspaper and magazine food columns. There's nothing like it anywhere, and we are very pleased with ourselves!

It is possible to cook a piece of meat just any old way. And lots of people do. If they are pleased with the results, then that was the right way to cook it. But alas, successful results from such a haphazard approach to cooking are rarely achieved. That is why we recommend an understanding of the basics in order to insure that the right cut, correct cooking method, proper timing, and budgets all fit together to provide the greatest satisfaction.

We are trying to help a meat shopper through the maze of meat cuts, meat-counter decisions, and cooking methods to make purchases that will provide family enjoyment and meet nutritional and entertainment needs. At the same time, we hope to help you solve problems which research has shown to be almost universal, including dealing with the person behind the meat counter.

We want to be sure you get what you pay for at the meat counter. Reading this book once and then referring to it occasionally will help you do just that.

No current major book on meat is more up-to-date. For example, the 1976 revisions of the United States Department of Agriculture in beef grade standards are fully covered in Chapter 1 in the section on the why and what of grading. Because few consumers have ever had much opportunity to learn about meat grades (or other food grades, for that matter) most readers will find this section particularly helpful and interesting.

After looking at this book's unique illustrated display of the most common meat cuts and names, you will know more than most people know about particular meat cuts, including what they look like and what they should be called. You will learn to recognize cuts even if the stores where you shop haven't yet adopted the URMIS system. You will be able to make better price and value comparisons and will know how to cook meat properly and to make the most of every dollar you spend for meat.

As with everything else, the basics come first. Then, whether you are a novice shopper or a veteran homemaker who has always been a bit hesitant about straying too far from the well-known, let the experimentation begin!

At a point late in this book's development, an acquaintance asked to whom it would be dedicated. Little attention had been given to such formality, but the question stirred up a thought. If it were to be dedicated, why not make it an offering with high hopes to butchers and homemakers, to corporate meat operations vice-presidents, and to unincorporated family managers—in the name of value given for dollars spent?

And so it is thus dedicated. May they go forward in common purpose!

David H. Stroud
President
National Live Stock & Meat Board
Chicago, 1977

The Meat Board Meat Book

1

The Basics of Buying Meat

From the days of the cavemen to the era of the astronauts, meat has been a favorite food. Although cavemen didn't know it, meat is also a highly nutritious food and an essential part of a healthy diet. An average $3\frac{1}{2}$ ounce (100 gram) serving supplies 52 percent of the daily protein requirements of the average adult male, a substantial amount of vitamins (31 percent of the thiamin requirements, 26 percent of the niacin requirements, and 22 percent of the riboflavin requirements), 36 percent of the iron requirements, and significant amounts of additional minerals. In addition to being nutritious, lean meat is low in calories.

Providing meat for dinner is easier today than it was in the caveman era. But even today it takes time and effort to learn how to buy meat properly and economically. Although consumerism is a fairly new word in the English language, its emergence and the happy fact that it is understood by so many people are clear indications American shoppers are becoming more sophisticated. Increasing numbers of people understandably refuse to spend hard-earned dollars unless they get full value for them.

The amount of money spent for meat represents approximately 25 percent of the average American weekly food budget, which would seem to indicate that a great many Americans find meals more satisfying when they include meat. Since meat represents such a substantial portion of our food budget and our diet, it makes good sense to take the time to learn how to buy meat properly, even if it requires homework.

A Helping Hand from Uncle Sam

The Federal Meat Inspection Act, passed in 1906, requires that all meat-packing plants engaged in interstate or foreign trade operate under federal inspection standards. The Federal Inspection Stamp attests to the wholesome quality of meat *but does not classify meat by grade.*

Although the original inspection act has been improved constantly over the years, the most significant improvement was the passage of the Wholesome Meat Act of 1967. This act requires that state inspection standards be equal to federal standards. Therefore, if a meat packer is not federally inspected, he falls under state guidelines. As a result, all meat sold commercially in the United States is inspected for wholesomeness by either federal or state authorities who use similar and very stringent guidelines.

Inspection of meat provides protection for the consumer by guaranteeing that all meat inspected and passed comes from healthy animals, which are slaughtered and processed under sanitary conditions. It also guarantees that the meat is suitable for consumption when it leaves the processing plant and that no labels carrying misleading statements appear on the meat. Additional evaluation and labeling are necessary to establish grade.

The familiar round USDA (United States Department of Agriculture) inspection stamp is made with a safe, edible, purple, vegetable dye which, in abbreviated form, proclaims "U. S. Inspected and Passed." The stamp includes the official number assigned by the government to each meat-packing plant. It is stamped on every carcass and must also be printed on all prepared-meat packages such as bacon and cold cuts.

Grading

The development and promotion of federal grading was initiated in 1927 by meat and animal scientists associated with the United States Department of Agriculture, scientists working with land grant colleges, and personnel of the National Live Stock & Meat Board. It is continued today by the United States Department of Agriculture. Grading was established to provide a uniform method of identifying those characteristics of meat that affect flavor and tenderness, and thus the dollar value. Since grading is directly related to the value of meat, its use provides an economic incentive for quality production.

There was no uniform system of identification for the different levels of quality in livestock and meat before grading was established. As a result, the farmer who produced top quality cattle received the same price in the marketplace as the farmer who produced cattle of lesser quality. This economic inequity followed down the line to the retailer, who received the same price for both top quality and lower quality meat. The introduction of grading provided farmers, packers, wholesalers, and retail distributors with uniform standards for buying and selling livestock and meat.

The acceptance of grading by all levels of customers developed as a natural outgrowth of a competitive economy. The most elegant hotels and restaurants, along with the then-exclusive dining car services, were encouraged to take advantage of grading and to select meat on a quality-grade basis. They discovered very quickly that meat of a given grade, unvarying in quality, could be purchased from almost any supplier. Many grocery and meat retailers followed suit and bought graded meat for their customers. The ability of these retailers to sell the same quality of meat day after day provided them with an edge in sales promotion and an increase in loyal customers.

Grading Is Voluntary

Meat grading is a service provided by the federal government, but paid for by meat packers. Participation in the program is voluntary. When requested, a federal grader comes to a meat plant (under contractual agreement) to evaluate those carcasses offered for grading. Once he has determined the correct grade, he applies the grade stamp. Graders are carefully trained. Most of them are college graduates with degrees in meat or animal science. All of them are government employees, not industry employees, and they, not the packers, decide the grade of every carcass evaluated. This system provides assurance to retail and food-service buyers and, ultimately, to the consumer that graded meat has been carefully evaluated by the United States Department of Agriculture and that the grade stamp visible on the carcass is correct.

Some packers and retailers, confident of their own ability to grade meat, prefer not to use or promote federal grades. They feel their own store, chain, or brand reputation is as valid as government grading and, in many cases, has earned customer confidence. However, there are a few cities where municipal law requires that all meat sold within city jurisdiction be federally graded. This ruling is intended to benefit consumers, but it also tends to restrict competition by eliminating some reliable retailers who sell firmly established quality "house brands."

Even when government grading is not officially used, the standards set by the USDA provide the criteria by which most meat is evaluated and priced.

How Meat Is Graded

Two basic considerations go into the grading of all meat. The first is a measurement of the proportion of the more desirable sections of a carcass or cut to the less desirable sections, along with a measurement of the ratio of meat to bone. The second consideration is an evaluation of the characteristics of meat associated with its potential for flavor and tenderness when properly cooked. Different kinds of meat require somewhat different approaches to measure these basic considerations.

Beef Grading   Beef is graded for both quality and yield.

Quality   A quality grade is an evaluation of the eating quality of meat. Beef quality grades are based on the following factors:

Marbling: The degree of marbling (flecks of fat in lean meat) is one of the most important factors affecting the quality of meat, particularly beef. Marbling increases juiciness, flavor, and tenderness and it is one of the qualities a consumer can evaluate easily, just by looking.

Maturity: The texture and color of meat, as well as the amount of bone ossification, are used to determine the maturity of a carcass. Increased maturity usually means decreased tenderness. Aging and maturity are not the same thing, at least where meat is concerned, and should not be confused with each other. Maturity relates to the chronological age of cattle. Aging is a natural tenderizing process that will be discussed later in this chapter.

Color, Firmness, and Texture: Bright color, firm lean, and fine texture are indications of high quality beef. These, too, are qualities consumers can judge for themselves.

Yield   The yield (or cutability) grade refers to the amount of usable meat in relation to the amount of fat and bone on a carcass. Yield grading was started in 1965 to encourage producers of livestock to work at improving their techniques of feeding and breeding in order to produce meatier animals. Although yield grade (see Chapter 3) is of no direct importance to the customer who buys a retail cut of meat, it is very important to anyone who buys a whole carcass, a side, or a wholesale cut.

Recent Changes in Beef Grading

Revisions have been made in the procedures for the grading of beef every decade or so since grading was first established in 1927. These revisions are required periodically to reflect changes in production management, genetic improvements of cattle breeds, and the changing availability of grain. The four revisions that went into effect in February 1976 were the first changes made since 1965. They are:

All beef that is graded must be graded for both quality and yield, not just one or the other. This rather technical revision does not directly affect the consumer who buys retail cuts of beef.

Conformation (the shape of a carcass) has been eliminated as a factor in determining the quality grade of beef. Under the old standards, and prior to recent improvements in cattle production, the shape or conformation of a beef carcass was very important because it provided a guide to yield. However, since yield grading provides a more accurate guide to the quantity of beef a carcass will provide, and since it has been shown conclusively that conformation does not affect quality at all, this factor has been eliminated in beef grading.

Slightly leaner beef will qualify as US Prime and US Choice. Marbling requirements (small flecks of fat sprinkled through the lean of beef) have been modified slightly. Previous marbling requirements were based on the fact that animals needed additional amounts of marbling as they matured to provide satisfactory levels of tenderness, juiciness, and flavor. Production-feeding improvements, new genetic developments, and cross-breeding have produced cattle that often reach market weight at less than twenty-four months of age. Research indicates that the tenderness, juiciness, and flavor of animals under thirty months old are not significantly affected by the maturing process. Therefore only minimum marbling requirements are necessary for a particular grade in animals less than thirty months old. Animals over thirty months are still required to have increasing amounts of marbling as they mature.

RELATIONSHIP BETWEEN MARBLING, MATURITY, AND QUALITY

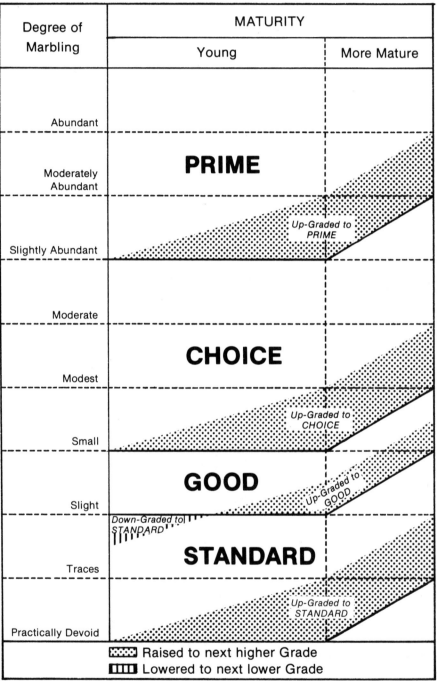

There are nine official degrees of marbling used for grading purposes. They are identified in the *Graders' Operating Manual* as: abundant, moderately abundant, slightly abundant, moderate, modest, small, slight, traces, and practically devoid. Because there are so many degrees of marbling, large quantities of beef will not arbitrarily be assigned significantly higher values. The amount of beef graded US Prime will probably rise by approximately 2 percent to a total of 6.5 percent. Over half of the graded beef has always been designated US Choice. This grade is likely to increase from the previous 54 percent, to between 64 and 68 percent.

Under the new grading system, cattle feeders will be able to cut back feeding time by at least two or three weeks. This will save more than five billion pounds of grain every year, and cattle breeders will still be able to provide tender, flavorful beef.

US Good has been redefined. Requirements for US Good grade have been tightened and made more restrictive. Although a very small percentage of beef previously graded Good will now qualify as Choice, there will also be a small percentage that will be downgraded to US Standard.

Veal, Lamb, and Pork Grading

The two factors that go into the grading of veal, lamb, and pork are quality and conformation.

The major difference between the quality grading of beef and that of veal, lamb, and pork is in the evaluation of intramuscular fat (marbling). Although marbling is important in the grading of lamb and pork, it is not evaluated in the same way as beef, and the terminology is different. Marbling is difficult to see in veal because the color of the lean is so light. However, in all three species, maturity, color, firmness, and the texture of the lean are evaluated in terms of their relationship to the ultimate flavor and tenderness of the meat.

Conformation is the term used to evaluate the general shape, form, and outline of a carcass. Superior conformation means a carcass has a thick back, full loins and ribs, deep plump rounds (legs), thick shoulders, and a short neck and shanks—not exactly the type of figure most women dream of having.

The Grades

Beef, veal, and lamb are graded from Prime (the highest grade) to Canner or Cull (the lowest grade). There are also federal grades for pork, but they are not widely used because pork is merchandised somewhat differently from other meat. Many cuts of pork, especially those that have been cured and smoked, carry packer brand names.

GOVERNMENT GRADES FOR BEEF, VEAL, LAMB, AND PORK

USDA Beef	USDA Veal	USDA Lamb	Pork
USDA Prime	USDA Prime	USDA Prime	U.S. No. 1
USDA Choice	USDA Choice	USDA Choice	U.S. No. 2
USDA Good	USDA Good	USDA Good	U.S. No. 3
USDA Standard	USDA Standard	USDA Utility	U.S. No. 4
USDA Commercial	USDA Utility	USDA Cull	Utility
USDA Utility	USDA Cull		
USDA Cutter			
USDA Canner			

USDA Prime is the top or highest grade of meat and contains the greatest degree of marbling. It is generally sold to the finer restaurants and to select meat stores. It is occasionally available in supermarkets and in unpretentious meat stores, but it is always the most expensive meat because it is produced in very limited quantities.

USDA Choice is sold in most retail stores and, over the past thirty years, has become the most popular grade of meat available. Although it is leaner than Prime, it still contains enough marbling to be flavorful and juicy and many cuts can be cooked quickly by dry heat. When a retail store sells USDA Choice it is usually advertised as such. Choice is also the grade that is distributed most widely to a very large percentage of the restaurant trade.

USDA Good contains less marbling than Choice and is not often offered as government graded meat. More often it is sold under a store brand or house brand name, or as economy meat. Some cuts may be cooked by the dry heat method, particularly if they have been marinated before cooking. This grade is as nutritious as the higher grades of meat but it is not as juicy, and the flavor is milder than that of the higher grades. (This is the grade often recommended for people on fat-restricted diets.)

USDA Standard is occasionally sold in retail stores under a store brand or house brand name. It is nutritious but less tender than the higher grades and most cuts must be cooked slowly by moist heat.

The remaining grades are not available in retail food stores. These grades are usually processed or ground and used in sausage, cold cuts, canned stew, luncheon loaf, or other manufactured meat products. Although lower grades are nutritious and wholesome, they lack the flavor and tenderness of higher grades. The more tender cuts (ribs and loins) are featured in many popular low-cost steak houses.

Once meat has been graded, the entire length of the carcass is stamped with the same safe vegetable dye used for the Inspection Stamp. It can be seen on untrimmed meat and occasionally is still visible on meat that has been cut and is ready for sale. If you have any questions about the grade of meat you are buying, ask your meat dealer to show you the grade stamp on the untrimmed carcass or wholesale cut.

Why Grading Is Important to the Consumer

Unfortunately the average consumer cannot look at a cut of meat and accurately determine the exact quality grade because there are so many factors that determine grade. Delicious and thoroughly satisfactory meals can be prepared using lower grades of meat, provided the meat is cooked correctly. But if you buy a lower grade and cook it by the wrong method, you may be disappointed when mealtime arrives because most cuts from the lower grades require slow cooking by moist heat in order to be tender and flavorful. It is therefore important to understand the various grades in order to know which grade to buy. It isn't always necessary, or even desirable, to buy the highest and most expensive grade. But it is always necessary to buy the correct grade for a specific cooking method.

Aging

Normally it takes from six to ten days to move fresh meat from packer to kitchen. This is long enough for considerable tenderizing to take place naturally because the enzymes always present in meat break down the meat fibers. The customer who prefers additional aging must be prepared to pay a premium price to a meat dealer who carries specially aged meat.

Usually only ribs and loins of high quality beef and lamb are aged. These cuts are already tender and the main purpose of aging is to develop additional tenderness and a special flavor. Meat suitable for aging must have a fairly thick covering of fat, in order to prevent undue discoloration and to keep the meat from drying out. Aged beef is often slightly darker in color than beef that has not been aged. Some weight loss and surface spoilage occur in aging, and this loss is one reason aged meat is expensive.

Meat is aged in one of three ways: the traditional dry-aging method, fast-aging or high temperature exposure, or aging in a vacuum package.

In the dry-aging method, meat is held from three to six weeks in controlled low-temperature (34° F to 38° F), low- or high-humidity conditions. Although this method may extend over a six-week period, most of the tenderization takes place within ten to fourteen days. Some meat experts use low humidity to keep meat surfaces dry. Others prefer high humidity to reduce evaporation loss.

Fast-aging is a method in which meat is held for two days or less in controlled high-temperature (about 70° F), high-humidity conditions. Ultraviolet lights are used to reduce bacterial growth.

Although vacuum packaging is not really an aging process, considerable tenderization takes place in the vacuum pack as the meat moves through normal distribution channels. Vacuum packaging also reduces the amount of shrinkage and surface spoilage.

Meat cannot be aged properly, safely, or adequately at home since temperature and humidity must be controlled at all times. Meat that has not been aged under the strictest controls may develop a higher bacterial count than is safe for human consumption.

Kosher meat may not be aged at all since, under traditional Jewish law, meat must be eaten within seventy-two hours of slaughtering.

Ground Beef—Fat Content the Important Factor

Unfortunately, many stores still label ground beef in the same way they have labeled it for years. "Ground sirloin," "ground round," "ground chuck," "hamburger," or just plain "ground beef" are typical labels. Sometimes there is a grade designation on the package, the higher grade commanding the higher price. Since the process of grinding tenderizes meat, it is unnecessary to pay extra to have an expensive, tender cut like sirloin ground, particularly if there is no way to know how much fat is added. The quality of ground beef is determined to a large extent by the ratio of lean meat to fat content.

In order to maintain good flavor and juiciness, ground beef should contain at least 15 percent fat. However, in no instance should it ever contain more than 30 percent fat. Since the fat-to-lean ratio is usually expressed as the percentage of lean, rather than the percentage of fat, look for ground beef that contains between 70 and 85 percent lean. The higher the fat content, the greater the cooking loss and, presumably, the lower the price. The problem is that the most inexpensive ground beef is not necessarily the most economical buy because of the high fat content that results in substantial cooking loss. Consumers who spend more to buy extra-lean ground beef will have more cooked meat to place on the table than consumers who buy the most inexpensive ground beef.

A few stores around the country are beginning to label ground meat "Not Less Than X% Lean." If your store does not label ground beef this way yet, ask the meat department manager to consider making the change. And, while you're speaking with him, ask him to tell you the lean-fat ratio in the ground beef you are about to purchase.

Meat labeled "ground beef" may not contain any pork, lamb, veal, or variety meat. When beef, pork, and veal are ground together they are labeled "ground meat loaf."

Two or Twelve for Dinner—How Much to Buy?

One of the most frequent questions customers ask their meat dealer is how much meat to buy. If your butcher is exceptionally knowledgeable and has enough ESP to judge the appetites of your family or guests, you may very well get a correct answer. But the chances are you will get an answer that reflects his own appetite, along with a simple, old-fashioned guess.

SERVINGS PER POUND TO EXPECT FROM A SPECIFIC CUT OF MEAT

The servings per pound listed in this table are based on an average serving of 2½ to 3½ ounces per portion. However, it should be noted that the yield of cooked lean meat is affected by the method of cooking, the degree of doneness, the size of the bone in bone-in cuts, and the amount of fat that remains after trimming.

BEEF

STEAKS

Chuck (Arm or Blade)	2
Cubed	4
Flank	3
Porterhouse	2
Rib	2
Rib Eye (Delmonico)	3
Round	3
Sirloin	2½
T-Bone	2
Tenderloin (Filet Mignon)	3
Top Loin	3

ROASTS

Rib	2
Rib Eye (Delmonico)	3
Rump Boneless	3
Tip	3

POT ROASTS

Chuck (Arm)	2
Chuck Blade	2
Chuck Boneless	2½
Cross Rib	2½

OTHER CUTS

Beef for Stew	4
Brisket	3
Ground Beef	4
Short Ribs	2

VARIETY MEATS

Brains	5
Heart	5
Kidney	4
Liver	4
Sweetbreads	5
Tongue	5

VEAL

CHOPS, STEAKS, CUTLETS

Loin Chops	3
Rib Chops	3
Round Steak	4
Shoulder Steaks	2½
Cutlets (Boneless)	5

ROASTS

Leg	3
Shoulder, Boneless	3

OTHER CUTS

Breast (Riblets)	2
Cubes	4

LAMB

CHOPS AND STEAKS

Leg Center Slice	4
Loin Chops	3
Rib Chops	3
Shoulder Chops	3
Sirloin Chops	3

ROASTS

Leg, Bone-in	3
Leg, Boneless	4
Shoulder, Bone-in	2½
Shoulder, Boneless	3

OTHER CUTS

Breast	2
Riblets	2
Cubes	4
Shanks	2

VARIETY MEATS

Heart	5
Kidney	5

PORK

CHOPS AND STEAKS

Blade Chops or Steaks	3
Boneless Chops	4
Loin Chops	4
Rib Chops	4
Smoked (Rib or Loin) Chops	4
Smoked Ham (Center Slice)	5

ROASTS

Leg (Fresh Ham), Bone-in	3
Leg (Fresh Ham), Boneless	3½
Smoked Ham, Bone-in	3½
Smoked Ham, Boneless	5
Smoked Ham, Canned	5
Blade Shoulder (Rolled) (Fresh or Smoked) Boneless	3
Blade Loin	2
Top Loin (Rolled) Boneless (Smoked or Fresh)	3½
Center Loin	2½
Smoked Loin	3
Arm Picnic Shoulder (Fresh or Smoked) Bone-in	2
Sirloin	2
Smoked Shoulder Roll	3

OTHER CUTS

Back Ribs	1½
Bacon (Regular), Sliced	6
Canadian-Style Bacon	5
Country-Style Back Ribs	1½
Cubes	4
Hocks (Fresh or Smoked)	1½
Pork Sausage	4
Spareribs	1½
Tenderloin (Whole)	4
Tenderloin (Fillets)	4

VARIETY MEATS

Brains, Heart, Kidney	5
Liver	4

You will be able to answer that question yourself—accurately and economically—when you understand the principles involved in estimating how much to buy.

Do you know how many portions you can expect to get from a pound of meat? A boneless, well-trimmed cut, such as a Beef Rib Eye Roast, will serve an average of three people per pound. On the other hand, well-trimmed Pork Loin Back Ribs will yield an average of only one and one-half servings per pound. Therefore, you must buy twice as many pounds of Back Ribs as Rib Eye Roast to feed the same number of people. You can see how the cut of meat you purchase, and how it is trimmed, are of major importance in determining how many pounds to buy.

The second factor to consider when deciding how much meat to buy is the cooking method you plan to use. There is more shrinkage in meat cooked at a high temperature than in meat cooked at a moderate temperature. The length of time meat is cooked is also a factor because there is more shrinkage in well-done meat than in meat that is cooked rare.

And finally, there are the questions of appetite, which obviously varies from person to person, and of how much additional food will be served with the meat.

The preceding table is based on an average portion of two and one-half to three and one-half ounces. Even if you serve larger or smaller portions, the chart provides an excellent guide to the relative amount of meat you can expect to get from many cuts.

Cost Per Serving, First Cousin of Cost Per Pound

Once you have begun to view a cut of meat in terms of how many portions it represents, in addition to how much it costs per pound, you have made a major step in learning to judge the true cost of meat. If that Rib Eye Roast is selling for $2.19 per pound, and you estimate it will serve three people per pound, each portion will cost 73 cents. If the Pork Loin Back Ribs sell for $1.19 per pound, and you estimate they will yield one and one-half servings per pound, each portion will cost 79 cents. Therefore, in spite of the fact that the Rib Eye Roast costs $1.00 per pound *more* than the Back Ribs, each portion of roast costs 6 cents *less* than the ribs. It is the more economical buy. Use the following table to compare the cost per serving for meat at various price levels.

COST FOR A SERVING OF MEAT AT VARIOUS PRICE LEVELS

Approximate Cost per Serving

COST PER POUND	1½ Servings per Pound	2 Servings per Pound	2½ Servings per Pound	3 Servings per Pound	3½ Servings per Pound	4 Servings per Pound	5 Servings per Pound	6 Servings per Pound
.59	.39	.30	.24	.20	.17	.15	.12	.10
.69	.46	.35	.28	.23	.20	.17	.14	.12
.79	.53	.40	.32	.26	.23	.20	.16	.13
.89	.59	.45	.36	.30	.25	.22	.18	.15
.99	.66	.50	.40	.33	.28	.25	.20	.17
1.09	.73	.55	.44	.36	.31	.27	.22	.18
1.19	.79	.60	.48	.40	.34	.30	.24	.20
1.29	.86	.65	.52	.43	.37	.32	.26	.22
1.39	.93	.70	.56	.46	.40	.35	.28	.23
1.49	.99	.75	.60	.50	.43	.37	.30	.25
1.59	1.06	.80	.64	.53	.45	.40	.32	.27
1.69	1.13	.85	.68	.56	.48	.42	.34	.28
1.79	1.19	.90	.72	.60	.51	.45	.36	.30
1.89	1.26	.95	.76	.63	.54	.47	.38	.32
1.99	1.33	1.00	.80	.66	.57	.50	.40	.33
2.09	1.39	1.05	.84	.70	.60	.52	.42	.35
2.19	1.46	1.10	.88	.73	.63	.55	.44	.37
2.29	1.53	1.15	.92	.76	.65	.57	.46	.38
2.39	1.59	1.20	.96	.80	.68	.60	.48	.40
2.49	1.66	1.25	1.00	.83	.71	.62	.50	.42
2.59	1.73	1.30	1.04	.86	.74	.65	.52	.43
2.69	1.79	1.35	1.08	.90	.77	.67	.54	.45
2.79	1.86	1.40	1.12	.93	.80	.70	.56	.47
2.89	1.93	1.45	1.16	.96	.82	.72	.58	.48
2.99	1.99	1.50	1.20	1.00	.85	.75	.60	.50

Where to Buy Meat

There are many places to purchase meat—speciality meat markets, farmers' markets, wholesale meat outlets, co-ops, mail-order houses that usually specialize in fancy meat, department stores with large food departments, and through a variety of food plan distributors. The most popular place to buy meat is in the supermarket, where the highest volume of retail meat is sold.

There is no question that many supermarkets have excellent meat departments, headed by knowledgeable meat cutters who maintain the highest possible standards. But hardly anyone would argue that this is always the case. Obviously the ultimate way to judge a meat department is to buy meat, cook it properly, and consider how it tastes. But there are other clues to the standards in different stores.

Is the meat packaged in see-through trays (and there *are* see-through trays that are biodegradable) so you can see both sides of the meat? Does the label supply information about the species or kind of meat (beef, veal, lamb, or pork), the primal or wholesale cut (chuck, round, shank, etc.), and the specific retail name of the cut (steak, rib roast, etc.)—or does the label only have a fanciful name designed to give you minimal information? Does the label include a cooking method? Does the label mention the grade of meat? Is the label placed over bone or fat to create the illusion that the meat is a better buy than it really is? Does the label have a clear understandable date? A store that packages meat so the consumer can see as much as possible, and labels packages clearly and informatively, is likely to be proud of the meat it sells.

The laws in a few states require that meat labels list species, primal cut, and retail name, and the day may come when all states will require this information. But a good meat department should include the information now, whether it is required by law or not.

A consumer should also be able to determine when a package of meat was wrapped. Laws vary from city to city regarding the dating of food. If the store where you shop uses a code instead of an understandable date, you can probably decipher the code by looking at the labels on ground meat. Ground meat must be freshly ground every day, and since the volume of sales is very high it is often ground several times a day. For example, in some areas a package of ground meat may have the numbers "95," or the letters "QR," where the date should be. The chances are these particular numbers or letters are the code for that day. Packaged meat is usually date-coded one way or another so the butcher knows exactly when it was wrapped, and he should be willing to share this information with you.

In any case, it's a good idea to remember that every supermarket has a department manager and a meat cutter. They are there to cut meat to your specifications, to trim meat properly, and to answer your questions. Get to know them. Develop the habit of asking if they recommend the packaged meat you have selected. You'd be surprised how often they may suggest another piece, or a different cut entirely.

Meat cutters are also available to help when the specific cut of meat you are looking for is nowhere in sight, or when you find the cut you want but not the weight you need. Very few supermarkets charge for service, even when it involves taking packaged meat from a case, recutting it at your request, and repackaging it. When a butcher performs this service, the price he puts on the repackaged meat should be exactly the same as the price on the original package, unless there is a prominently posted sign stating that there is a service charge.

How to Read the Weight on a Label

The label on meat shows weight in pounds simply and clearly, but it usually shows fractions of a pound as a decimal rather than in ounces. You know how many pounds of meat you are buying, but figuring the ounces can be confusing since the weight that follows the decimal point is shown in hundredths of a pound. At 16 ounces to a pound, each ounce is a little over six one-hundredths of a pound. By looking at the chart below you will be able to see that if the net weight on a meat label reads 4.40, it means your meat weighs 4 and 40/100 pounds, or 4 pounds and 6.4 ounces, *not* 4 pounds and 4 ounces. One-half pound is 8 ounces; the label will read ".50;" 4 ounces will be shown as ".25." Once you have that relationship firmly established, you should be able to determine the correct weight of any piece of meat reasonably accurately.

Number after Decimal (hundredths of a pound)		Equivalent Weight in Ounces
.10		1.6
.20		3.2
.25	One-Quarter Pound	4.0
.30		4.8
.40		6.4
.50	One-Half Pound	8.0
.60		9.6
.70		11.2
.75	Three-Quarters Pound	12.0
.80		12.8
.90		14.4
1.00	One Pound	16.0

The Bent Truth in Advertising

Laws, both state and federal, prohibit merchants from making statements in advertisements that are deliberate lies. But a distressing number of stores manage to skirt the law by using advertising gimmicks that leave the truth thoroughly bent and battered. It's unfortunate how many times an advertisement for meat is essentially truthful but at the same time manages to be misleading.

The key word in the advertisement shown here is in the top line—"untrimmed." When a whole loin is trimmed there is a weight loss of between one third and one half of the original weight. If you purchase a 21 pound *untrimmed* loin for $1.59 per pound, it will cost $33.39. In the unlikely event you are very lucky, and the trimming loss is only one third, you will take home 14 pounds of usable meat. If you pay $33.39 for the 14 pounds you actually take home, each pound will really cost $2.385. That means you save only half a cent per pound

WHOLE OR HALF UNTRIMMED BEEF LOIN

LOIN of BEEF

Buy a whole or half loin and we'll custom slice it to your specifications . . . into steaks, roasts or half and half . . . with extras for your freezer.

1^{59}
LB. 18 TO 22 LBS. AVG. WGT.

WELL TRIMMED BEEF LOIN

LOIN STEAKS . . . . LB. **2**^{39}

Typical misleading advertisement

by buying a whole loin. There isn't an untruthful word in the entire ad. But the implication of the ad is that you will save a lot of money by buying a whole or half loin, instead of buying individual top loin steaks. If you succumb to the ad and buy a whole loin, the store will have succeeded in moving extra inventory from its shelves to your freezer; but you will not have saved money. On the other hand, if your weight loss is much more than one third, it will actually cost more money per pound to buy a half or whole untrimmed loin than it will cost to buy individual top loin steaks.

Advertisements often gratuitously proclaim that the meat being sold is "naturally aged." The assumption is that the consumer will see the word "aged" and jump to the conclusion that the meat has been specially aged. The fact is that all meat ages "naturally" as it moves from packer to store.

If a store advertises the grade of meat it is selling, the grade designation must be preceded by the initials USDA. Therefore, if a store wants you to know it is selling Choice Grade, the advertisement will read USDA Choice. However, many stores that do not sell Choice try to get around this ruling by using the words "Your Choice" or "Choice of." If you read an ad very quickly, you may be left with the impression that the advertisement is for Choice Grade meat. What the advertisement should really tell you is that the meat is *not* Choice. If it were, it would say USDA Choice.

One remarkable ad recently read "Sirloin Steaks," followed in small print by the statements: "More sirloin beef for your money." (More than what?) "Undesirable tail and tail fat removed." (The tail and tail fat are *always* removed from a sirloin steak. It is the tail of a Porterhouse Steak that is sometimes left on.) "Fillet removed." (Those are the key words, and they tell you the steaks are from the hip and all the loin has been removed.) One can only assume the advertiser hopes the consumer will not actually read all of the ad since it certainly is no favor to remove the fillet!

There are too many examples of deceptive ads. Your only method of protection from them is knowledge. Know what you are buying and read ads carefully, particularly for what they do *not* say.

Assertiveness Can Save Money

Timidity and uncertainty in a supermarket can be expensive. The most effective way to shop is to view the meat counter as a challenge. The store manager and the meat cutter are both eager to sell you as much meat as possible at the best possible price. You, the shopper, should be determined to buy only what you want and need for as reasonable a price as possible. When the quality of meat you buy is not up to standard, take it back. When a store advertises meat on sale, but runs out of it before you get to the store, get a "rain check" that will allow you to buy the same meat at the sale price when supplies are replenished. If you can't find the cut of meat you want, or the weight you need, ask for it. If you have a question about the weight marked on a package of meat, use the store scales to check. If your meat has not been properly trimmed, ask the meat cutter to trim it for you.

An assertive shopper need not be an unpleasant person, merely a determined and knowledgeable consumer. But most of all, an assertive shopper is not anonymous. Get to know your meat dealer. Tell him your name and find out what his name is. Ask his advice and help. Above all, if you are prepared to tell him when meat is not up to standard, be sure you tell him when meat is exceptionally good.

2

Know Your Meat

The decisions you make at the meat counter are the most important choices you make when you market. Menus usually are planned around meat dishes, balanced diets depend on them, and food budgets often are determined by them.

With over three hundred cuts of beef, veal, pork, and lamb to choose from, it's understandable why so many consumers are frustrated and confused. Even though no store is ever likely to offer all three hundred cuts at one time, the number offered can still be bewildering. But it is possible to buy meat with ease and confidence if you understand why one cut is different from another and therefore know what you want, what you are buying, and how to prepare it.

Starting on page 42 you'll find full-color photographs and complete descriptions of 166 retail cuts of beef, veal, lamb, and pork. The standard meat identification names are shown, along with often-found common names for the cuts. These particular cuts were selected for inclusion because they represent the most popular and most frequently purchased cuts sold in the United States today.

You'll profit from your expanded knowledge of meat by being able to choose cuts you have never used before, perhaps because you were uncertain what they were or how they should be prepared. When proper cooking methods are followed, there's little need to worry about failure in the kitchen, even when you try a cut of meat for the first time.

Food dollars will stretch further when you can select economical cuts of meat. These are less in demand than the more familiar cuts, but they are potentially equal in appetite appeal and nutritional value.

Successful meat shopping begins at home. Try to plan menus in advance and set out with a general idea of what you want to buy. You can determine how much meat you'll need by figuring the number of people to be served and then estimating how many servings a cut of meat will provide. Consult the table in Chapter 1 for help in making these determinations. Remember, a boneless cut yields more servings per pound than a bone-in or bony cut. Be flexible about menus so you can adjust your meal planning to take advantage of meat sales, or make a substitution if a particular cut of meat does not seem to be a good buy.

The diagrams of the four species of animals shown in this chapter will help you become familiar with the wholesale or primal cuts. There are photographs of the most popular retail cuts. Each cut is accompanied by its complete name, the fanciful names that have been used for years, a general description of the cut, and the proper cooking method or methods.

Once you're at the meat counter, let the label on each package of meat be your shopping guide. It can eliminate guesswork if it tells you the species or kind of meat (beef, pork, lamb, or veal), primal or wholesale cut, and retail cut.

The Uniform Retail Meat Identity Standards program, which was developed by the National Live Stock & Meat Board in response to consumer need, is responsible for the new methods used to label meat. This system, adopted by a majority of meat retailers across the country, has standardized the names of retail cuts. When they are used, you need not worry that the same cut of meat will have a variety of different names in different stores or in different parts of the country. Nor will you be puzzled by misleading fanciful names.

Buying meat is an important job. You are likely to face it at least once a week. When you are familiar with meat cuts, know what they look like, where they come from, and how to cook them, you can make expert decisions at the meat counter. You can't afford not to.

Choosing the Right Grade *and* the Right Cut

If you buy a top grade of meat and cook it properly there is no reason why you will not have a successful meal. But if you plan to serve a pot-roast, for example, it is a foolish extravagance to buy heavily marbled Prime. The major advantage of Prime is that it can be cooked by dry heat (broiling, pan-broiling, pan-frying, or roasting) and it will be tender. Since slow gentle cooking in liquid tenderizes meat, you can save money by purposely buying a lower grade when you intend to braise or cook in liquid.

In the same way that higher grades of meat cost more than lower grades, certain cuts of meat cost more than other cuts. A Beef Round Eye Round Roast is delicious roasted. It can also be braised. But it makes much more sense to buy something like a Beef Chuck Shoulder Pot-Roast to braise because it costs less per pound. Cuts that can be cooked by dry heat can also be cooked by slow moist heat, but buying them is unnecessarily expensive. The reverse, however, is not true. A less tender cut that should be braised will not be tender (unless it has been pretendered) if it is oven-cooked as a roast. This chapter lists the cuts of meat available throughout the country along with the recommended cooking methods. Consult it before you decide which cut to buy, in order to avoid buying a more expensive cut than you need for a recipe.

"Too Much" Can Cost Less Than "Just Enough"

A ham steak cut from the center of a smoked ham commands a premium price. However, if you buy a Smoked Ham Rump Half and ask the butcher to slice a few steaks from it, you will pay less per pound for the steaks because you only pay the price per pound of the less expensive Rump Half. There are many instances where you can save money by buying a large piece of meat and having the meat cutter slice some of it off for use as a separate meal. Among your choices are pork chops and kabobs that can be cut from a pork roast and beef steaks from a standing rib roast. You can get lamb chops from a roast or leg of lamb, veal chops and steaks from veal roasts, and cubes for a casserole or stew and ground beef from one end of a pot-roast.

A close look at the meat cuts listed in this chapter will give you a simplified view of where many higher priced cuts come from. Small families often pass up large cuts of meat because they don't want to eat the same meat several nights in a row. But if you learn how to divide a large roast by cutting it into a small roast, a few steaks, and some kebobs, you can have three entirely different meals from one large cut of meat. And of course you can always freeze a portion of the meat for use several weeks later.

Beef

Beef cattle are the largest meat animals. They are marketed when they are at least eight months old, although the average age is between twelve and twenty-two months.

The bright, cherry-red color of beef makes it easy to identify. Streaks or flecks of fat intermingled throughout the lean (marbling) contribute to flavor and tenderness. There may be less fat or marbling in beef from young cattle than in meat from more mature animals but young beef is usually more tender because of its age.

A beef carcass is divided into halves, called sides, for ease in handling. Each side is divided into a forequarter and a hindquarter. The quarters are further broken down into the wholesale or primal cuts shown on the diagram.

Beef is finally divided into the retail cuts available at a meat counter. There are seven basic groupings of retail beef cuts: blade cuts and arm cuts (both from the chuck), rib cuts, loin cuts, sirloin cuts, round cuts, and breast cuts (brisket and plate).

The location of wholesale cuts gives you a clue to the tenderness of the retail cut. The most tender cuts are from the lightly-used muscles of the rib and short loin. The more active muscles of the chuck and round yield the less tender cuts, which, because of their relative abundance, are lower in price.

The cooking method you use determines the final tenderness of the meat. This is why it is so important to choose the proper cooking method, particularly for the more economical, less tender cuts. Knowing the wholesale cut, you will be able to evaluate the tenderness of a retail cut and choose the proper cooking method. Tender cuts should be cooked by dry heat. The less tender cuts, unless they have been pretendered, *must* be cooked by moist heat.

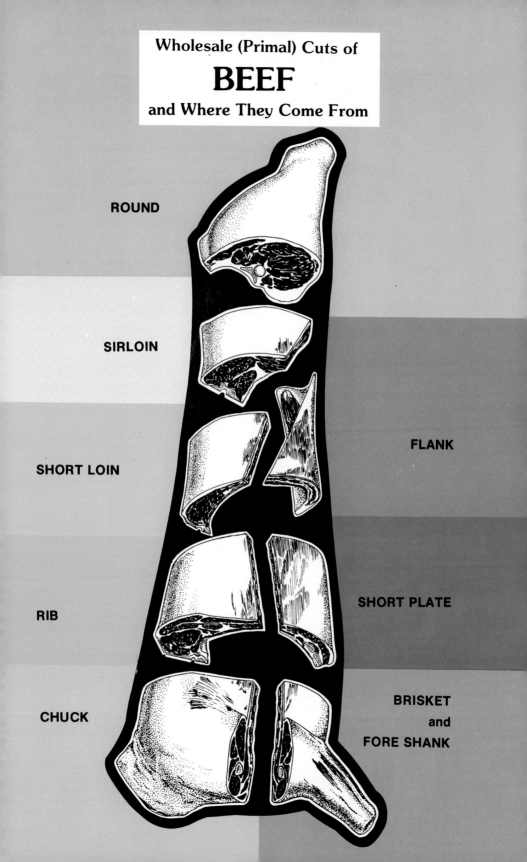

Wholesale (Primal) Cuts of
BEEF
and Where They Come From

ROUND

SIRLOIN

FLANK

SHORT LOIN

RIB

SHORT PLATE

CHUCK

BRISKET
and
FORE SHANK

Beef Chuck Arm Pot-Roast

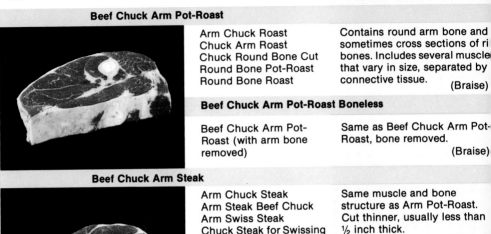

Arm Chuck Roast
Chuck Arm Roast
Chuck Round Bone Cut
Round Bone Pot-Roast
Round Bone Roast

Contains round arm bone and sometimes cross sections of ri bones. Includes several muscle that vary in size, separated by connective tissue.
(Braise)

Beef Chuck Arm Pot-Roast Boneless

Beef Chuck Arm Pot-Roast (with arm bone removed)

Same as Beef Chuck Arm Pot-Roast, bone removed.
(Braise)

Beef Chuck Arm Steak

Arm Chuck Steak
Arm Steak Beef Chuck
Arm Swiss Steak
Chuck Steak for Swissing
Round Bone Steak
Round Bone Swiss Steak

Same muscle and bone structure as Arm Pot-Roast. Cut thinner, usually less than ½ inch thick.
(Braise)

Beef Chuck Arm Steak Boneless

Boneless Arm Steak
Boneless Round Bone Steak
Boneless Swiss Steak

Same as Beef Chuck Arm Steak bone removed.
(Braise)

Beef Chuck Shoulder Pot-Roast Boneless

Boneless English Roast
Cross Rib Roast, Boneless
Honey Cut
Shoulder Roast
Shoulder Roast, Boneless

Part of arm portion of chuck. Boneless, with very little fat cover.

(Braise)

Beef Chuck Shoulder Steak Boneless

English Steak
Shoulder Steak
Shoulder Steak, Boneless
Shoulder Steak, Half Cut

Same muscle structure as Be Chuck Shoulder Pot-Roast. Boneless, cut thinner.

(Braise)

Beef Chuck Cross Rib Pot-Roast

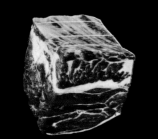

Boston Cut
Bread and Butter Cut
Cross Rib Roast
English Cut Roast
Thick Rib Roast

Cut from the arm half of beef chuck. Square cut, thicker at o end, containing two or three bones and alternating layers lean and fat. May be tied.
(Braise)

Beef Chuck Cross Rib Pot-Roast Boneless

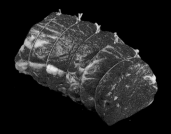

ut from arm half of chuck.
quare cut, bones removed.
ean contains several thin layers
fat. Tied to keep shape.

Boneless Boston Cut
Boneless English Cut
Cross Rib Roast, Boneless
English Roll

(Braise)

Beef Chuck Short Ribs

ectangular-shaped,
ternating layers of lean and fat.
ontain rib bones, cross
ctions of which are exposed.

Barbecue Ribs
Braising Ribs
English Short Ribs,
    Extra Lean
Short Ribs

(Braise, Cook in Liquid)

Beef Chuck Flanken Style Ribs

ut lengthwise, rather than
tween ribs as short ribs.
ntain rib bones and
ternating streaks of lean
d fat.

Barbecue Ribs
Braising Ribs
Brust Flanken
Flanken Short Ribs
Kosher Ribs

(Braise, Cook in Liquid)

Beef For Stew

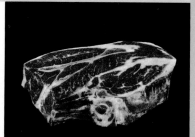

ay be cut from chuck, brisket,
, or plate. Meaty pieces
ntain varying amounts of fat,
t into 1- to 2-inch squares.

Beef Cubed for Stew
Boneless Beef for Stew
Boneless Stew Beef

(Braise, Cook in Liquid)

Beef Chuck Blade Roast

ntains blade bone, backbone,
bone, and a variety of
scles. Usually cut about 2
hes thick.

Blade Chuck Roast
Chuck Blade Roast
Chuck Roast Blade Cut
Chuck Roast First Cut

(Braise, Roast)

Recommended Names for Retail Cuts Often Used Names	**Descriptions of Cuts**

Beef Chuck Blade Steak

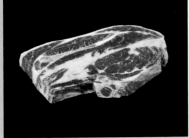

Blade Steak
Chuck Blade Steak
Chuck Steak Blade Cut
Chuck Steak, First Cut

Same as Beef Chuck Blade Roast, cut thinner.

(Braise, Broil, or Panbroil)

Beef Chuck 7-Bone Pot-Roast

Center Cut Pot-Roast
Chuck Roast Center Cut
7-Bone Roast

Cut from center of the blade portion of chuck. Identified by 7-shaped blade bone. Contain backbone, rib bone, and a variety of muscles.

(Braise)

Beef Chuck 7-Bone Steak

Center Chuck Steak
Chuck Steak Center Cut
7-Bone Steak

Same muscle and bone structure as Beef Chuck 7-Bor Pot-Roast. Cut thinner, usuall less than 1½ inches thick.

(Braise)

Beef Chuck Top Blade Pot-Roast

Blade Roast, Bone-in
7-Bone Roast
Top Chuck Roast

Contains short 7-shaped blad bone and two or three muscle from top portion of blade roa Fat covering on one side.

(Braise)

Beef Chuck Top Blade Steak

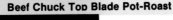

Blade Steak, Bone-in
Top Blade Steak
Top Chuck Steak, Bone-in

Same as Beef Chuck Top Blade Pot-Roast, cut 1 inch thinner.

(Braise)

Beef Chuck Under Blade Pot-Roast

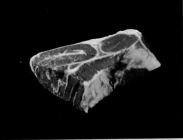

Bottom Chuck Roast
California Roast
Semiboneless Roast
Under Cut Roast

Contains bones and muscles bottom portion of blade roast including chuck eye muscles and rib bone.

(Braise, Roast)

Beef Chuck Under Blade Steak

Same muscle and bone structure as Beef Chuck Under Blade Pot-Roast. Cut thinner, usually less than 1½ inches thick.

(Braise, Broil, Panbroil, Panfry)

Bottom Chuck Steak
California Steak
Semiboneless Chuck
    Steak
Under Cut Steak

Beef Chuck Under Blade Pot-Roast Boneless

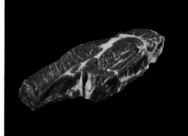

Bones removed from Beef Chuck Under Blade Pot-Roast, leaving chuck eye, several other muscles, and narrow streaks of fat.

(Braise, Broil, Panbroil, Panfry)

Boneless Roast Bottom
    Chuck
Bottom Chuck Roast,
    Boneless
California Roast
    Boneless
Inside Chuck Roast

Beef Chuck Under Blade Steak Boneless

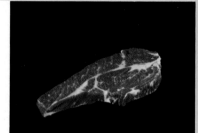

Same muscle structure as Beef Chuck Under Blade Pot-Roast Boneless. Cut thinner, usually less than 1½ inches thick.

(Braise, Broil, Panbroil, Panfry)

Boneless Chuck Steak
Bottom Chuck Steak,
    Boneless
Chuck Fillet Steak
Under Cut Steak Boneless

Beef Chuck Mock Tender

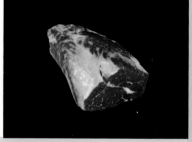

Cut from above blade bone. Naturally boneless, consisting of a single tapering muscle with minimal fat covering.

(Braise)

Chuck Eye
Chuck Fillet
Chuck Tender
Fish Muscle
Medallion Pot-Roast
Scotch Tender

Beef Chuck Top Blade Roast Boneless

Triangular-shaped cut taken from above blade bone. Naturally boneless, with large amount of connective tissue.

(Braise)

Flat Iron Roast
Lifter Roast
Puff roast
Shoulder Roast Thin End
Triangle Roast

Beef Chuck Top Blade Steaks Boneless

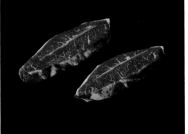

Book Steak
Butler Steak
Lifter Steak
Petite Steak
Top Chuck Steak,
   Boneless

Same muscle structure as Beef
Chuck Top Blade Roast
Boneless, cut into thin slices.
Steaks are oval-shaped with
minimal fat covering.

(Braise, Panfry)

Beef Chuck Eye Roast Boneless

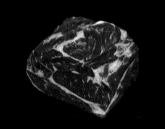

Boneless Chuck Roll
Boneless Chuck Fillet
Chuck Eye Roast
Inside Chuck Roll

Contains meaty inside muscles
of blade chuck, some seam fat
and thin fat cover, if any.

(Braise, Roast)

Beef Chuck Eye Steak Boneless

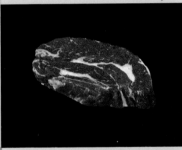

Boneless Chuck Fillet
   Steak
Boneless Steak Bottom
   Chuck
Chuck Boneless Slices
Chuck Eye Steak
Chuck Fillet Steak

Same muscle structure as Beef
Chuck Eye Roast Boneless,
sliced.

(Braise, Broil, Panbroil, Panfry)

Beef Shank Cross Cuts

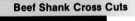

Center Beef Shanks
Cross Cut Shanks
Fore Shank for Soup
   Meat, Bone-in

Cut from hindshank or
foreshank, perpendicular to
bone, 1 to 2½ inches thick.

(Braise, Cook in Liquid)

Beef Brisket Point Half Boneless

Brisket Front Cut
Brisket Point Cut
Brisket Thick Cut

Brisket (breast) section,
between foreshank and plate.
Contains layers of fat and lean
but no bones. May be cured in
salt brine (pickling) to make
Corned Beef Brisket.

(Braise, Cook in Liquid)

Beef Brisket Flat Half Boneless

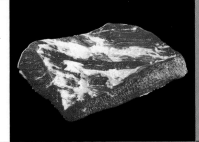

Brisket (breast) section. Cut from rear portion of lean and fat closest to plate layers. Breast and rib bones removed. May be cured in salt brine (pickling) to make Corned Beef Brisket.

Brisket First Cut
Brisket Flat Cut
Brisket Thin Cut

(Braise, Cook in Liquid)

Beef Plate Skirt Steak Boneless

"Skirt" is inner diaphragm muscle.

Skirt Steak
Diaphragm

(Braise, Broil, Panbroil, Panfry)

Beef Plate Skirt Steak Rolls Boneless

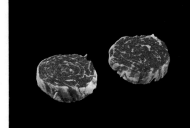

"Skirt" is inner diaphragm muscle with elongated muscling. Usually sliced ¾ to 1 inch thick, rolled to form pinwheels and either tied or skewered.

Beef London Broil
London Broils
Skirt Fillets
Skirt London Broils
London Grill Steak

(Braise, Broil, Panbroil, Panfry)

Beef Flank Steak

Boneless flat oval-cut containing elongated muscle fibers and very little fat. Surface may be scored.

Flank Steak Fillet
Plank Steak
London Broil
Jiffy Steak

(Broil, Braise)

Beef Flank Steak Rolls

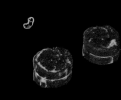

Flank Steak, rolled and secured with ties or skewers, cut crosswise into ¾- to 1-inch slices.

Beef London Broils
Cubed Flank Steak
Flank Steak Fillets
Flank Steak London
    Broils
London Broils

(Braise, Broil, Panbroil, Panfry)

Beef Rib Roast Large End

Beef Rib Pot-Roast,
Short Cut 6-7
Standing Rib Roast 6-7
Beef Rib Roast, Short
Cut 6-7
Rib Roast Oven Ready

Cut from large end of rib primal ribs six to nine, or any combination of two or three ribs Contains large eye muscle with elongated muscling, streaked with strips of fat that surround rib eye. Good fat covering. Cut at rib six.

(Roast)

Beef Rib Roast Small End

Rib Roast Oven Ready
Standing Rib Roast
Sirloin Tip Roast

Cut from small end of primal rib Contains large rib eye muscle and two or more ribs.

(Roast)

Beef Rib Steak Small End

Beef Rib Steak
Beef Rib Steak, Bone-in

Same as Rib Roast Small End, usually cut 1 inch thick or less.

(Broil, Panbroil, Panfry)

Beef Rib Steak Small End Boneless

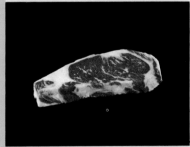

Beef Rib Steak, Boneless
Spencer Steak, Boneless

Same as Rib Steak Small End, rib bone removed.

(Broil, Panbroil, Panfry)

Beef Rib Eye Roast

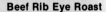
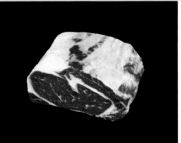

Delmonico Pot-Roast
Delmonico Roast
Beef Rib Eye Pot-Roast
Regular Roll Roast

Large center muscle of rib (rib eye). All other muscles, bones, and seam fat removed.

(Roast)

Beef Rib Eye Steak

Cut across grain from Beef Rib Eye Roast. Little or no fat cover.

Delmonico Steak
Boneless Rib Eye Steak
Fillet Steak
Spencer Steak
Beauty Steak

(Broil, Panbroil, Panfry)

Beef Loin Top Loin Steak

Contains top loin muscle and backbone running length of cut. Tenderloin removed. Outside fat covering.

Shell Steak
Strip Steak
Club Steak
Chip Club Steak
Bone-in Club Sirloin
  Steak
Country Club Steak
Sirloin Strip Steak,
  Bone-in
(Broil, Panbroil, Panfry) Delmonico Steak

Beef Loin Top Loin Steak Boneless

Same as Beef Loin Top Loin Steak, backbone removed.

Strip Steak
Kansas City Steak
N. Y. Strip Steak
Sirloin Steak, Hotel
  Style
Beef Loin Ambassador
  Steak
Beef Loin Strip Steak,
  Hotel Cut
(Broil, Panbroil, Panfry) Boneless Club Sirloin
  Steak

Beef Loin T-Bone Steak

Derives name from T-shape of finger bone and backbone. Contains top loin and tenderloin muscles. Tenderloin is smaller in Beef Loin T-Bone Steak than in Beef Loin Porterhouse Steak. (Diameter of tenderloin no less than ½ inch when measured across center.)

T-Bone Steak

(Broil, Panbroil, Panfry)

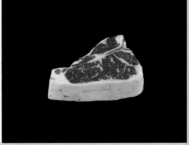

Beef Loin Porterhouse Steak

Contains top loin, tenderloin muscles, backbone, and finger bone. Similar to Beef Loin T-Bone Steak, but tenderloin is larger. (Diameter of tenderloin no less than 1¼ inches when measured across center.)

Porterhouse Steak

(Broil, Panbroil, Panfry)

Beef Loin Wedge Bone Sirloin Steak*

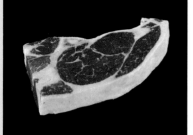

Beef Sirloin Steak,
   Wedge Bone
Beef Sirloin Steak,
   Short Cut
Sirloin Steak

Contains portion of backbone
and hip bone. Varies in bone an▪
muscle structure depending o▪
location in sirloin section of loin▪
Shape of hip bone resembles
wedge.

(Broil, Panbroil, Panfry)

Beef Loin Round Bone Sirloin Steak*

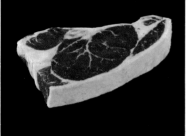

Sirloin Steak

Contains portion of backbone
and muscle structure. Largest
muscles include top sirloin an▪
tenderloin, interspersed with fa▪
Shape of hip bone resembles
round bone.

(Broil, Panbroil, Panfry)

Beef Loin Flat Bone Sirloin Steak*

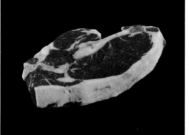

Beef Sirloin Steak,
   Flat Bone
Sirloin Steak
Flat Bone Sirloin
   Steak

Contains top sirloin and
tenderloin muscles. Hip bone
shape is long and flat.

(Broil, Panbroil, Panfry)

Beef Loin Pin Bone Sirloin Steak*

Beef Sirloin Steak,
   Pin Bone
Sirloin Steak

Contains top sirloin and
tenderloin muscles. Also
includes backbone and portio▪
of hip bone, which vary in size▪

(Broil, Panbroil, Panfry)

Beef Loin Shell Sirloin Steak

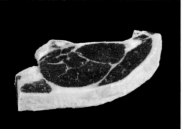

Beef Sirloin
N. Y. Steak Bone-in
N. Y. Sirloin Steak

Similar to other Beef Loin Sirlo▪
Steaks, tenderloin muscle is
removed.

(Broil, Panbroil, Panfry)

*May be referred to as Beef Loin Sirloin Steak.

Beef Loin Sirloin Steak Boneless

Same as Beef Loin Sirloin Steak, bones removed. Muscle structure varies.

Sirloin Steak Boneless
Rump Steak

(Broil, Panbroil, Panfry)

Beef Loin Top Sirloin Steak Boneless

Beef Loin Sirloin Steak, bones and tenderloin removed.

Top Sirloin Steak

(Broil, Panbroil, Panfry)

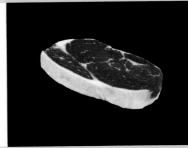

Beef Loin Tenderloin Roast

Cut from tenderloin muscle. Elongated with rounded large end, gradually tapering to thin, flat end. Boneless, with little if any fat covering. Very tender.

Beef Tenderloin Tip
    Roast
Beef Tenderloin,
    Filet Mignon Roast
Beef Tenderloin,
    Châteaubriand

(Roast, Broil)

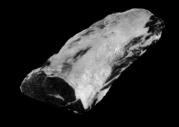

Beef Loin Tenderloin Steaks*

Cut across grain from Beef Loin Tenderloin Roast. Probably most tender steak in carcass.

Filet Mignon
Beef Fillet Steak
Beef Tenderloin
    Fillet DeBoeuf
Beef Tender Steak

(Broil, Panbroil, Panfry)

*May be referred to as Beef Loin, Filet Mignon.

Beef Round Steak

Lean, oval-shaped cut containing round bone and three major muscles: top, bottom, and eye of round. Thin fat covering on outer edges.

Beef Round Steak
Beef Round Steak,
    Center Cut
Beef Round Steak,
    Full Cut

Beef Round Steak Boneless

Same as Beef Round Steak, bone removed.

(Braise, Panfry)

Beef Round Steak
Beef Round Steak,
    Center Cut Boneless
Beef Round, Full Cut

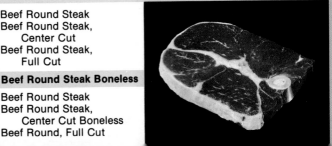

Beef Round Rump Roast

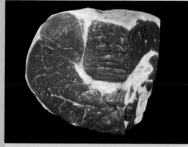

Beef Round Rump Roast
 Bone-in
Beef Round Standing
 Rump

Contains aitchbone and three
major round muscles: top
round, eye of round, and
bottom round. Fat covering on
outer surface.

(Braise, Roast)

Beef Round Rump Roast Boneless

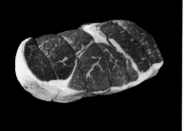

Beef Round Boneless
 Rump
Beef Round Rump Roast,
 Rolled

Same as Beef Round Rump
Roast, bone removed. Usually
tied.

(Braise, Roast)

Beef Round Heel of Round

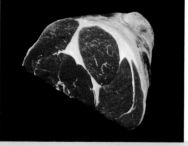

Beef Roast Heel
 Pot-Roast
Pike's Peak Roast
Diamond Roast
Denver Pot-Roast
Horseshoe Roast

Boneless, wedge-shaped cut,
containing top, bottom, and eye
round muscles. Least tender cut
of round. Has considerable
connective tissue.

(Braise, Cook in Liquid)

Beef Round Top Round Roast

Beef Top Round Roast
Beef Top Round Roast,
 Center

Contains inside top muscle of
round. Boneless, with small
amount of fat on outer surface.

(Roast)

Beef Round Top Round Steak

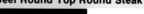

Beef Top Round Steak
Beef Top Round Steak,
 Center Cut

Same muscle structure as Beef
Round Top Round Roast, cut
thinner.

(Broil, Panbroil, Panfry)

Beef Round Bottom Rump Round Roast

Irregular-shaped, thick cut, from outside (or bottom) of round. Comes from sirloin end of bottom round. Slight fat covering.

(Braise, Roast)

Round Tip Roast
Round Back of Rump
    Roast

Beef Round Bottom Round Roast

Thick cut from outside of round. Irregular shape, elongated muscling, slight fat covering.

(Braise, Roast)

Beef Bottom Round
    Pot-Roast
Beef Bottom Round
    Oven Roast
Beef Bottom Round Steak
    Pot-Roast

Beef Round Eye Round Roast

Cut from eye round muscle, which has been removed from bottom round. Elongated, naturally boneless, slight fat covering.

(Braise, Roast)

Beef Eye Round Roast
Beef Round Eye
    Pot-Roast
Eye Round Pot-Roast
Beef Round Eye Roast

Beef Round Eye Round Steaks

"Eye" is smallest muscle and is round, elongated, and naturally boneless. Steaks cut crosswise from "eye" muscle have slight fat covering.

(Braise, Panbroil, Panfry)

Eye Round Steak
Beef Round Eye Steak

Beef Round Tip Roast

Wedge-shaped cut from thin side of round. Contains cap muscle of sirloin.

(Braise, Roast)

Beef Sirloin Tip Roast
Face Round Roast
Tip Sirloin Roast
Round Tip Roast
Crescent Roast

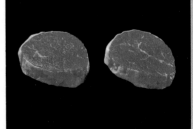

Beef Round Tip Roast Cap Off

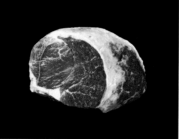

Ball Tip Roast
Full Trimmed Tip Roast

Same as Beef Round Tip Roast
bone, cap muscle, and thin layer
of outer fat removed. Compact
and easy to carve.

(Braise, Roast)

Beef Round Tip Steak Cap Off

Ball Tip Steak
Trimmed Tip Steak

Boneless cut with only slight
amount of outer fat. Cap muscle
removed. Usually very lean.

(Broil, Panbroil, Panfry)

Beef Round Cubes for Kabobs

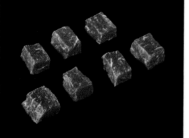

Beef Sirloin Tip,
   Kabob Cubes

Lean pieces of round cut into
cubes. Usually taken from
meatiest muscles, such as tip.

(Braise, Broil)

Beef Cubed Steak

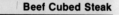

Cube Steak

Square- or rectangular-shaped.
Cubed effect made by machine
that tenderizes mechanically.
May be made from muscles of
several primal cuts.

(Braise, Panfry)

Ground Beef

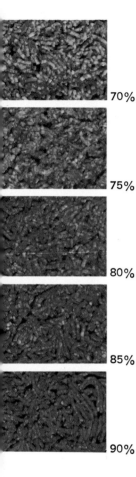

70%

75%

80%

85%

90%

From roadside restaurant to family kitchen, ground beef or "hamburger" is a major part of the American diet. But in spite of its great popularity, there is nothing sold at the meat counter that causes as much confusion and misunderstanding as ground beef.

Fresh ground beef is sold as "ground chuck," "ground round," "ground sirloin," "hamburger," or just plain "ground beef." The obvious reason for such a variety of names is that sometimes the meat that is ground comes from a specific section of carcass. However, the most important factor in ground beef is the lean-to-fat ratio of the meat, not the basic differences in tenderness found in cuts from various sections of a carcass. When no additional fat is added to meat during grinding, meat from the round is the most lean. "Ground chuck" is not as lean as "ground round." "Ground sirloin" falls between the round and the chuck in fat content.

The lean content of ground beef should never be less than 70 percent. On the other hand, the leanest ground beef would have to contain approximately 10 to 15 percent fat for flavor and for ease in cooking. Some meat stores have already begun to label ground beef according to the lean-to-fat ratio, and it is to be hoped that all ground beef eventually will be labeled in this way.

The only accurate way the lean-to-fat ratio can be judged is through scientific measurement. But it is possible to make some judgment by looking at the meat carefully or by measuring the amount of fat drippings rendered when meat is cooked.

Veal

Veal is the meat from calves that are not older than three months, which weigh 350 pounds or less, and which have had a diet of milk and little, if any, roughage. Although veal is limited in supply, and therefore relatively expensive per pound, there is almost no waste in most retail cuts. As a result, the cost per serving can be very reasonable.

Veal should be fine-grained, velvety in texture, and light pink in color. Because veal comes from such young animals, it is always very lean.

The wholesale and retail cuts of beef and veal are similar. Veal is simply smaller.

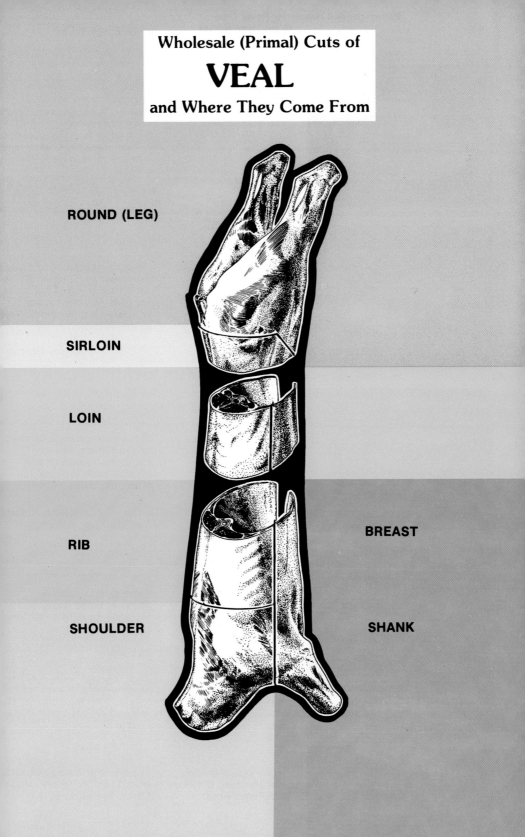

Veal Shoulder Arm Roast

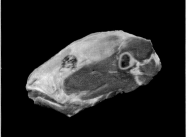

Veal Shoulder Roast
Veal Round Bone Roast

Shoulder cut containing arm bone, rib bones from underside and cross sections of bones exposed on face side. Muscles include shoulder, forearm, and thin layer of lean meat from brisket.

(Braise, Roast)

Veal Shoulder Arm Steak

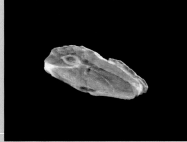

Veal Round Bone Steak
Veal Shoulder Steak

Same structure as Veal Shoulder Arm Roast, cut thinner. Cross sections of arm and rib bones exposed. Muscles include shoulder, forearm, and thin layer of lean brisket.

(Braise, Panfry)

Veal Shoulder Blade Roast

Veal Shoulder Roast
Veal Blade Roast

Contains blade bone exposed on cut surface, ribs, and backbone from underside. Muscles include chuck, top blade, and chuck tender.

(Braise, Roast)

Veal Shoulder Blade Steak

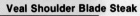

Veal Shoulder Steak
Shoulder Veal Chops

Same structure as Veal Shoulder Blade Roast, except for thickness. Contains blade bone, backbone, and, depending on thickness, a rib bone.

(Braise, Panfry)

Veal Shoulder Roast Boneless

Rolled Veal Shoulder
Veal Shoulder, Boneless
Veal Rolled Roast

Shoulder cut, bones removed. Rolled and tied to keep shape. Slight covering exposed.

(Braise, Roast)

Veal Breast

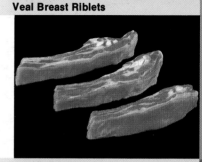

Rear portion of foresaddle. Contains lower ribs. Quite lean with some fat layered within lean. Elongated muscling. Scant fat covering.

(Braise, Roast)

Breast-of-Veal
Veal Breast

Veal Breast Riblets

Long narrow cuts containing rib bones and slight fat covering. Some connective tissue layered within lean.

(Braise, Cook in Liquid)

Veal Riblets

Veal for Stew

Meaty pieces cut into 1- to 2-inch squares. May be cut from shoulder, shank, or round.

(Braise, Cook in Liquid)

Stew Veal
Veal Stew (large pieces)
Veal Stew (small pieces)
Veal Stew, Boneless

Veal Rib Roast

Contains ribs six to twelve, rib eye muscle, featherbones, and part of chine bone. Does not contain tenderloin.

(Roast)

Veal Rib Roast
Rib Veal Roast

Veal Rib Chops

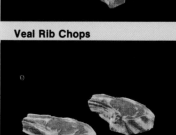

Contains featherbone, part of chine bone, and, depending on thickness, rib bone. Largest muscle is rib eye.

(Braise, Panfry)

Veal Chops
Veal Rib Chops
Rib Veal Chops

Veal Rib Crown Roast

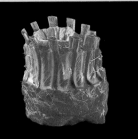

Veal Crown Roast
Veal Crown Rib Roast

Cut from half of primal rib. Contains ribs six to twelve which have rib bones trimmed 1 to 2 inches from end. Ribs curved and tied to resemble crown when roast rests on backbone.

(Roast)

Veal Loin Roast

Veal Loin Roast

Contains top loin and tenderloin muscles, backbone, and T-shaped fingerbone.

(Roast)

Veal Loin Chops

Veal Chops
Veal Loin Chops
Loin Veal Chops

Contain backbone and fingerbone. Muscles include top loin and tenderloin. Tenderloin differentiates this chop from rib chop. Size of chops gets smaller as chops near rib.

(Braise, Panfry)

Veal Loin Kidney Chops

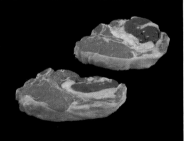

Veal Kidney Chops
Kidney Veal Chops

Contain backbone and featherbones. Muscles contained are loin and tenderloin. Side includes kidneys. Cut contains cross-sectional cut of kidney attached by kidney fat.

(Braise, Panfry)

Veal Loin Top Loin Chops

Veal Chops
Boneless Veal Chops

Same as Veal Loin Chops, tenderloin removed.

(Braise, Panfry)

Veal Leg Sirloin Roast

Contains portion of hip bone, backbone, and variety of muscles.

Veal Sirloin Roast

(Roast)

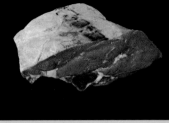

Veal Leg Sirloin Roast Boneless

Boneless roast, rolled and tied to keep shape. Lean, covered with small amount of outside fat.

Rolled Double Sirloin
    Roast
Boneless Sirloin Roast

(Roast)

Veal Leg Sirloin Steak

Contains portion of backbone and hip bone. Size and shape of muscles and bones vary with each steak.

Veal Steak
Veal Sirloin Steak
Sirloin Veal Chop

(Braise, Panfry)

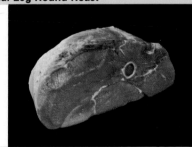

Veal Leg Round Roast

Cone-shaped with round leg bone exposed. Contains top, bottom, and eye muscles.

Veal Leg Roast
Leg of Veal

(Braise, Roast)

Veal Leg Round Steak

Cut from center of leg. Contains top, bottom, eye muscles, and cross section of leg bone. Has thin outer covering of fat and skin.

Veal Scallopini
Veal Steak
Veal Steakettes

(Braise, Panfry)

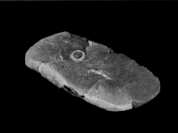

Recommended Names for Retail Cuts		
	Often Used Names	**Descriptions of Cuts**

Veal Leg Rump Roast

Veal Rump Roast
Rump of Veal

Contains three major round muscles: top round, eye round and bottom round, separated by connective tissue. Also contains aitchbone and fat covering on outer muscle. Irregularly shaped roast.

(Braise, Roast)

Veal Leg Rump Roast Boneless

Rolled Rump Roast
Veal Roast Boneless
Rump of Veal Boneless

Boneless roast. Usually rolled and tied to make compact. Easy to carve. Fat covering on outside of roast.

(Braise, Roast)

Veal Cubed Steaks

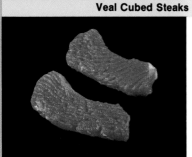

Veal Cubed Steak
Cubed Veal Steak

Can be made from any boneless lean cut of leg. Identified by square or rectangular appearance. Cubed effect made by a machine that tenderizes mechanically. Steaks made from several pieces of meat. All cuts have appearance of a single piece.

(Braise, Panfry)

Veal Cutlets

Veal Cutlets

Thin, boneless slices from leg. Very lean.

(Braise, Panfry)

Veal Cutlets Thin Sliced

Veal Cutlets

Thin, boneless slices, about ½ inch thick. From rear leg. Very lean.

(Braise, Panfry)

Ground Veal

Lean meat and trimmings
mechanically ground. Sold in
bulk or patty form.

Ground Veal

(Braise, Panfry, Roast)

Pork

The pork sold today comes from improved hogs that have been selected and bred to produce leaner cuts of meat. These hogs are marketed when they are five to nine months old.

Pork may be purchased in many forms—fresh, cured (pickled), cured and smoked, or canned. About 35 percent of the pork sold is fresh; the remaining 65 percent is cured or is used in manufactured meat products, such as sausage. The color of pork ranges from the grayish-pink of fresh pork to the delicate rose color of cured pork.

Pork sold today is younger, leaner meat than it used to be, and therefore it is more tender. It can be prepared by dry-heat cooking, such as broiling and roasting, if the cooking temperature is carefully controlled. Fresh pork should be cooked slowly to an interior temperature of 170° F for maximum flavor and juiciness. You can be certain it is thoroughly cooked when the meat is a gray color throughout and no trace of pink remains.

There are two types of cured-and-smoked pork cuts, "fully-cooked" and "cook-before-eating." The label on the wrapped meat should clearly identify which type it is. If there is no label on the meat, assume the cut has only been smoked and must be cooked before it is eaten.

Cook-before-eating hams have already been heated to an internal temperature of at least 140° F during smoking. This temperature destroys trichina (which is rarely present). But, for the best flavor and maximum tenderness, these hams should be cooked before serving. Fully-cooked hams have been smoked and cooked to an internal temperature of at least 150° F. They do not require further cooking unless you want to serve them hot.

The label "ham, water added," which appears on many types and styles of ham, can be confusing. Cuts that carry this label have been pumped with a curing solution and then smoked. If enough moisture does not evaporate during the smoking process to reduce the ham to its original fresh weight, the ham is labeled "water added." These hams may contain up to 10 percent added moisture.

Although pork is small enough to transport easily in uncut form, it is usually broken down at the packing plant. (Many pork cuts such as ham and sausage are processed before they reach the meat counter.) Pork is shipped to local retailers in the wholesale cuts shown on the diagram.

LEG (HAM)

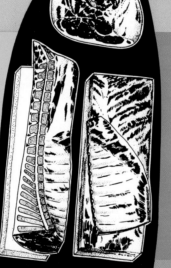

**BACON
(SIDE PORK)**

LOIN

SPARERIBS

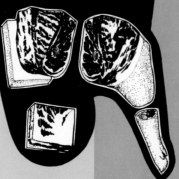

**BOSTON
SHOULDER**

**PICNIC
SHOULDER**

JOWL

Pork Shoulder Arm Picnic

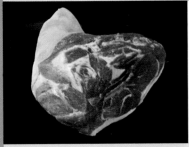

Fresh Picnic
Picnic
Whole Fresh Picnic
Pork Picnic Shoulder

Contains arm bone, shank bone
and portion of blade bone.
Shoulder muscles interspersed
with fat. Shank and part of lower
area covered with skin.

(Roast)

Pork Shoulder Arm Roast

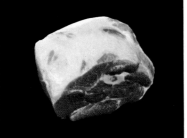

Pork Arm Roast
Fresh Pork Arm Roast

Cut from Arm Picnic. Shank
removed, leaving round arm
bone and meaty part of Arm
Picnic. Outside covered with
thin layer of fat.

(Roast)

Pork Shoulder Arm Steak

Arm Steak
Picnic Steak
Fresh Picnic Steak

Same muscle and bone
structure as Pork Shoulder Arm
Picnic, cut thinner.

(Braise, Panfry)

Pork Shoulder Blade (Boston) Roast

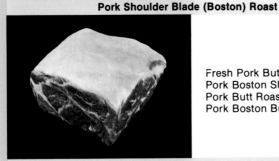

Fresh Pork Butt
Pork Boston Shoulder
Pork Butt Roast
Pork Boston Butt Roast

Top portion of whole shoulder.
Contains blade bone, exposed
on two sides. Some
intermuscular fat.

(Roast)

Pork Shoulder Blade (Boston) Roast Boneless

Boneless Pork Butt
Pork Boston Shoulder,
   Boneless
Boneless Pork Butt
   Roast
Boneless Rolled Butt Roast
Boneless Boston Roast

Same as Pork Shoulder Blade
(Boston) Roast, blade bone
removed. Usually tied with string
or placed inside elastic netting.

(Roast)

Pork Shoulder Blade Steak

...ut from Pork Shoulder Blade ...oston Roast. Contains blade ...one and several muscles.

Blade Pork Steak
Pork Loin 7-Rib Cut
Pork Steak

(Braise, Broil, Panbroil, Panfry)

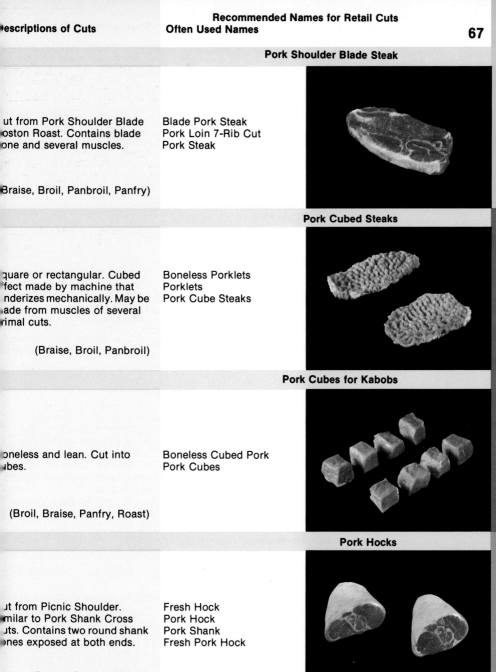

Pork Cubed Steaks

...quare or rectangular. Cubed ...fect made by machine that ...nderizes mechanically. May be ...ade from muscles of several ...rimal cuts.

Boneless Porklets
Porklets
Pork Cube Steaks

(Braise, Broil, Panbroil)

Pork Cubes for Kabobs

...oneless and lean. Cut into ...ubes.

Boneless Cubed Pork
Pork Cubes

(Broil, Braise, Panfry, Roast)

Pork Hocks

...ut from Picnic Shoulder. ...milar to Pork Shank Cross ...ts. Contains two round shank ...nes exposed at both ends.

Fresh Hock
Pork Hock
Pork Shank
Fresh Pork Hock

(Braise, Cook in Liquid)

Pork Loin Blade Roast

...ontains part of blade bone, rib ...nes, and backbone. Large loin ...e muscle surrounded by ...veral smaller muscles.

Pork Loin 7-Rib Roast
Pork Loin 5-Rib Roast
Rib End Roast
Rib Pork Roast
Pork Loin Rib End

(Roast)

Pork Loin Blade Chops

Blade Pork Chops
Pork Loin Blade Steaks
Pork Chops End Cut

Cut from blade end of loin.
Contains same muscle and bon
structure as Pork Loin Blade
Roast.

(Braise, Broil, Panbroil, Panfry

Pork Loin Country Style Ribs

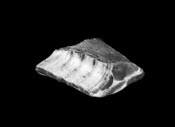

Country Style
　Spareribs
Country Ribs
Blade End Country
　Spareribs

Made by splitting blade end of
loin into halves lengthwise.
Contains part of loin eye muscl
and either rib bones or
backbones.

(Roast, Bake, Braise,
Broil, Cook in Liquid)

Pork Loin Back Ribs

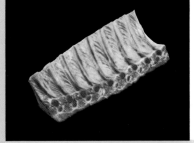

Pork Backribs
Loin Back Ribs
Country Back Bones
Pork Ribs for Barbecue

Cut from blade and center
section of loin. Contain rib
bones. Meat between ribs calle
finger meat. Layer of meat
covering ribs comes from loin
eye muscle.

(Roast, Bake, Braise,
Broil, Cook in Liquid)

Pork Loin Center Rib Roast

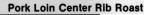

Center Cut Pork Roast
Pork Loin Rib Half
Pork Loin Center Cut
Pork Loin Roast
Loin Roast Center Cut

Cut from center rib area of loi
Contains loin eye muscle and
rib bones.

(Roast)

Pork Loin Rib Chops*

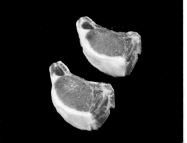

Rib Cut Chops
Rib Pork Chops
Pork Chops End Cut

Contain loin eye muscle and
backbone. Rib bone may be
present, depending on
thickness. Fat covering on
outside edge.

(Braise, Broil, Panbroil, Panfr

*May be called Center Cut Chops.

Pork Loin Rib Chops for Stuffing

ontain rib eye muscle and rib
one. Backbone present. No
enderloin.

Pocket Pork Chops
Pork Chops Stuffed

Braise, Broil, Panbroil, Panfry)

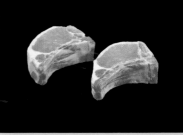

Pork Loin Center Loin Roast

ut from center of loin. Contains
b eye, tenderloin muscles, rib
ones, T-shaped bones. Thin fat
overing.

Pork Roast
Center Cut
Center Cut Pork Loin
   Roast
Center Cut Loin Roast
Loin Roast Center Cut

(Roast)

Pork Loin Top Loin Chops

ontain top loin muscles and
ackbone running length of cut.
enderloin removed. Outside
t covering.

Center Cut Loin Pork
   Chops
Center Cut Loin Chops
Strip Chops

Braise, Broil, Panbroil, Panfry)

Pork Loin Butterfly Chops

ouble chop, about 2 inches
ick, from boneless loin eye
uscle. Sliced almost in half to
rm two sides resembling
utterfly.

Boneless Butterfly Pork
   Chops
Butterfly Pork Chops

Braise, Broil, Panbroil, Panfry)

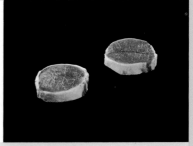

Pork Loin Top Loin Roast Boneless (Double)

wo boneless loins reversed and
ed together with fat side out
make boneless roast.

(Roast)

Boneless Roast From
   Pork Loins
Boneless Pork Loin
   Roast
Pork Loin Roast, Boneless

Recommended Names for Retail Cuts	Often Used Names	Descriptions of Cuts

Pork Loin Chops

Pork Chops
Loin End Chops
Loin Pork Chops
Center Loin Chops

Cut from sirloin end of loin. Eye muscle and tenderloin divided by T-shaped bone. Also contains backbone.

(Braise, Broil, Panbroil, Panfry)

Pork Loin Sirloin Roast

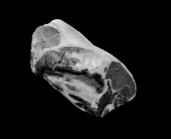

Loin End Roast
Loin Pork Roast
Sirloin End Roast
Hipbone Roast

Contains hip bone and backbone. Largest muscle is eye of loin, separated from smaller tenderloin muscles by finger bones.

(Roast)

Pork Loin Sirloin Chops

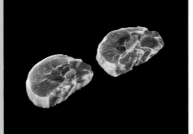

Pork Sirloin Chops
Sirloin Pork Chops
Sirloin Pork Steaks

Cut from sirloin end of loin. Same muscle and bone structure as Pork Loin Sirloin Roast.

(Braise, Broil, Panbroil, Panfry)

Pork Loin Sirloin Cutlets

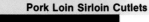
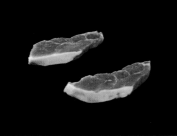

Pork Cutlets

Boneless slices cut from sirloin end of loin after tenderloin, hip bone, and backbone are removed.

(Braise, Broil, Panbroil, Panfry)

Pork Loin Tenderloin Whole

Pork Tender
Pork Tenderloin

Boneless cut taken from inside of loin. Largest end is round in shape and gradually tapers to the thin flat end. Very tender.

(Roast, Bake, Braise, Broil)

Pork Loin Tenderloin Pieces

Lean cubes of tenderloin.
Scant fat content. Very tender
lean cuts.

Pork Loin Tender-
loin Pieces

(Braise, Broil, Roast)

Pork Spareribs

Cut from side. Contain long rib
bones with thin covering of meat
on outside and between ribs.
May contain rib cartilage.

Fresh Spareribs
Pork Spareribs Fresh

(Roast, Bake, Broil,
Cook in Liquid)

Fresh Side Pork

Same cut as Slab Bacon but
fresh, from section of side that
remains after loin and spareribs
are removed. Layered lean from
fat generally used as seasoning.

Chunk Side of Pork
Fresh Side Pork
Fresh Belly
Streak of Lean

(Cook in Liquid)

Pork Leg (Fresh Ham) Whole

Hind Leg bone-in. Usually
covered with skin and fat about
halfway up leg.

Pork Leg Whole
Fresh Ham
Pork Leg Fresh Ham
Whole

(Roast)

Pork Leg (Fresh Ham) Roast Boneless

Same as Pork Leg (Fresh Ham).
Whole, all bones and skin
removed. May be tied or placed
in elastic netting.

Rolled Fresh Ham
Pork Leg Roast Boneless
Fresh Ham Boneless

(Roast)

Pork Leg (Fresh Ham) Shank Portion

Pork Leg Shank
    Portion
Fresh Ham Shank
    Portion
Pork Leg Roast Shank
    Portion

Lower portion of leg. Contains shank bone and part of femur bone. Skin covers shank and small portion of outside muscle

(Roast, Cook in Liquid)

Pork Pieces

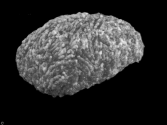

Pork Pieces

Lean cubes. May be taken from any meaty section of fresh mea

(Braise, Broil, Panfry, Roast)

Ground Pork

Ground Pork

Unseasoned, ground, from wholesale cuts which are generally in limited demand. Also made from lean trimming Sold in bulk form.

(Broil, Panbroil,
Panfry, Roast, Bake)

Smoked Pork Shoulder Picnic Whole

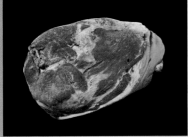

Picnic Shoulder
Smoked Picnic
Smoked Picnic Shoulder
Smoked Callie

Same muscle and bone structure as fresh Pork Should Arm Picnic. Cured and smoke

(Roast, Bake, Cook in Liquid)

Smoked Pork Shoulder Roll

Shoulder Roll
Smoked Shoulder Butt
Smoked Pork Shoulder
    Butt, Boneless
Cottage Butt
Daisy Ham

Cured and smoked, meaty, boneless eye of Pork Shoulde Blade Boston Roast.

(Roast, Bake, Cook in Liquid)

Smoked Pork Hocks

ontain two round shank bones
xposed at both ends. Oval-
haped, 2 to 3 inches thick.
ured and smoked.

Smoked Hock
Smoked Ham Hocks
Ham Hocks, Smoked

(Braise, Cook in Liquid)

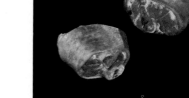

Smoked Pork Loin Canadian Style Bacon

ade from boneless loin. Cured
nd smoked. Single elongated
uscle with little fat.

Canadian Bacon
Back Bacon

(Roast, Bake if sliced,
Broil, Panbroil, Panfry)

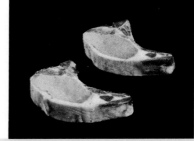

Smoked Pork Loin Rib Chops

ame muscle and bone
ructure as fresh Pork Loin Rib
hops. Cured and smoked.

Smoked Pork Chops
Smoked Rib Pork Chops
Center Cut Pork Chops
  Smoked

(Roast, Bake,
Broil, Panbroil, Panfry)

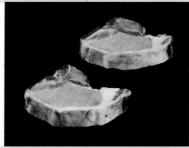

Smoked Pork Loin Chops

ame muscle and bone
ructure as fresh Pork Loin
hops. Cured and smoked.

Smoked Pork Chops
Smoked Loin Pork Chops
Center Cut Pork Chops
  Smoked

(Roast, Bake,
Broil, Panbroil, Panfry)

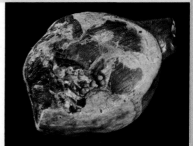

Smoked Ham Whole

ame muscle and bone
ructure as Pork Leg (Fresh
am) Whole. Cured and
noked.

Whole Ham, Smoked

(Roast, Bake)

Smoked Ham Shank Portion

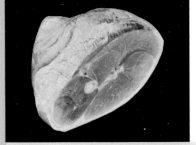

Ham Shank End
Shank Portion Ham
Ham, Shank Portion

Same muscle and bone
structure as Pork Leg (Fres
Ham) Shank Portion. Cured an
smoked.

(Roast, Bake)

Smoked Ham Rump Portion

Ham Sirloin End
Ham Butt Portion
Ham Butt End

Portion of cured and smoke
ham that contains aitchbone an
part of leg bone. Thin fat cove
on outer surface.

(Roast, Bake)

Smoked Ham Center Slices

Ham Center Slices
Cooked Ham Center
  Slices
Ham, Center Slices

Cut from center portion of
cured, smoked ham. Contain
top, bottom, tip muscles, an
round bone.
(Broil, Panbroil,
Panfry, Roast, Bake)

Smoked Ham Boneless Center Slices

Boneless Centers
Ham Slice, Boneless

Same as Smoked Ham Center
Slices, without bone.
(Broil, Panbroil,
Panfry, Roast, Bake)

Slab Bacon

Smoked Slab Bacon
Slab Bacon

Cured and smoked side.
Contains streaks of lean and fa
on one side. Other side may b
covered with skin.

(Broil if sliced,
Panbroil, Panfry, Roast, Bake)

Sliced Bacon

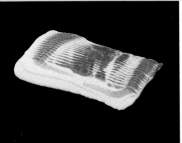

Smoked Sliced Bacon
Sliced Bacon

Sliced from Slab Bacon. May b
shingled. Outer skin removed.

(Broil, Panbroil,
Panfry, Roast, Bake)

Made from ground, fresh meat and seasonings such as salt, pepper, and sage. Stuffed in casings and shaped into links.

Sausage Links

(Braise, Panfry, Roast, Bake)

Lamb

If you enjoy eating meat that has a delicate flavor and is very tender, try lamb. At one time, lamb was available only in the spring. Happily, lamb is now available year-round. For best flavor, lamb is usually marketed when it is about six to eight months old. The color is pinkish-red.

When lamb reaches its first birthday, it becomes mutton, which is more popular in Europe than in the United States. Cuts of mutton are similar to lamb but are larger in size and darker in color. The meat is less tender, has more fat, and is less delicate in flavor than lamb. When available, it is also likely to be less expensive than lamb.

Prestige cuts such as rib crown roast, rib frenched chops, and rib roast have given lamb an expensive reputation. However, many cuts are in less demand and therefore are economical and are ideal to use for adding variety to menus. Cuts from the shoulder—shoulder arm roast, shoulder blade roast, and lamb for stew—are good examples of the less expensive cuts available that can provide delicious budget-stretching meals. You'll be able to identify and evaluate different cuts by understanding the relationship of wholesale and retail cuts shown on the diagram.

Wholesale (Primal) Cuts of
LAMB
and Where They Come From

LEG

SIRLOIN

LOIN

RIB

SHOULDER

NECK

BREAST

and

FORE SHANK

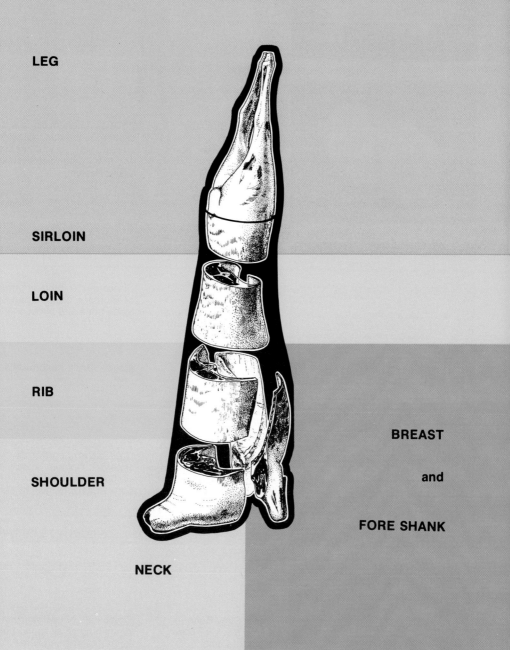

Lamb Shoulder Square Cut Whole

Shoulder Block
Shoulder Roast
Square Cut Shoulder

Square-shaped cut containing arm, blade, and rib bones. Thin paper-like outside covering is called "fell."

(Roast)

Lamb Shoulder Roast Boneless

Boneless Shoulder
Netted
Rolled Shoulder Roast

Boneless cut from blade and arm section of shoulder. Outside covered with fat and fell. Rolled and tied for compactness and ease of carving.

(Roast)

Lamb Shoulder Blade Chops

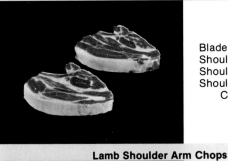

Blade Cut Chops
Shoulder Blocks
Shoulder Lamb Chops
Shoulder Blade Lamb
    Chops

Chops cut from blade portion of shoulder. Contain part of blade bone and backbone.

(Braise, Broil, Panbroil, Panfr

Lamb Shoulder Arm Chops

Shoulder Blocks
Lamb Round Bone Chops
Shoulder Chops
Arm Cut Chops

Cut from arm portion of shoulder. Contain cross section of round arm bone and rib bones.

(Braise, Broil, Panbroil)

Lamb Shoulder Neck Slices

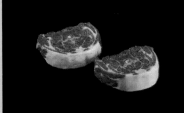

Lamb Stew Bone-in
Lamb Neck for Stew
Neck of Lamb
Lamb Neck Pieces

Cross cuts of neck portion containing small round bone. Lean interspersed with connective tissue.

(Braise

Lamb Breast

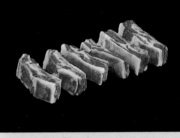

Part of forequarter, containing ribs. Oblong in shape with layers of fat within lean. Generally fat covering on one side.

Breast of Lamb

(Braise, Roast)

Lamb Breast Riblets

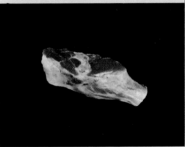

Cut from breast, containing ribs with meat and fat in layers. Cuts are long and narrow.

Lamb Riblets
Lamb Riblets Breast

(Braise, Cook in Liquid)

Lamb Shank

Cut from arm of shoulder. Contains leg bone and part of round shoulder bone. Covered by thin layer of fat and fell.

Lamb Fore Shank
Lamb Trotter

(Braise, Cook in Liquid)

Lamb Rib Roast

Contains rib bones, backbone, and thick, meaty, rib eye muscle. Fell usually removed.

Lamb Rib Rack for
　Roasting
Lamb Rack Roast
Hotel Rack

(Roast)

Lamb Rib Chops

Contain backbone and, depending on thickness, a rib bone. Meaty area is rib eye muscle. Outer surface covered by fat with fell removed.

Rack Lamb Chops
Lamb Rib Chops
Fresh Lamb Rib Chops
Rib Lamb Chops

(Broil, Panbroil,
Panfry, Roast, Bake)

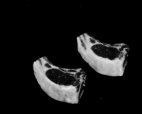

Lamb Rib Crown Roast

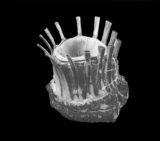

Lamb Crown Roast

Cut from half of rib. Rib bone trimmed 1 to 2 inches from end. Ribs curved and secured to resemble crown when roasts sits on backbone.

(Roast)

Lamb Loin Chops

Lamb Loin Chops
Loin Lamb Chops

Contains part of backbone. Muscles include the eye of the loin (separated from the tender loin by T-shaped finger bones) and the flank. Kidney fat on top of tenderloin and outer surface covered with fat; fell removed.

(Broil, Panbroil, Panfry)

Lamb Loin Double Chops

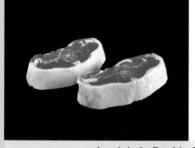

Double Chops
English Chops

Flank removed from cut. Contain top loin (larger muscle) and tenderloin (smaller muscle). Cut is "double" because it is a cross cut of loin containing both sides of carcass.

(Broil, Panbroil, Panfry)

Lamb Loin Double Chops Boneless

English Chop
Boneless Double
Loin Chop

Bone removed from loin double chop and cut, rolled pinwheel fashion, and secured to make compact, boneless chop.

(Broil, Panbroil, Panfry)

Lamb Leg Sirloin Chops

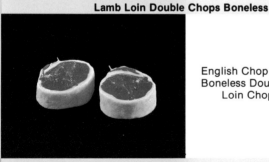
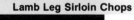

Sirloin Lamb Chop
Lamb Sirloin Steak

Cut from sirloin section of leg. Contains backbone and part of hip bone, which vary in shape with each chop. Muscles include top sirloin, tenderloin, and flank. Fat on outside, fell removed.

(Broil, Panbroil, Panfry)

Lamb Leg Whole

Contains sirloin section with hip bone, and shank portion with round bone. Outside covered with fell.

Leg, Sirloin On
Leg-o-Lamb
Leg of Lamb-Oven Ready
Full Trimmed Leg Roast

(Roast)

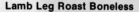

Lamb Leg Roast Boneless

All leg bones removed. Lean is rolled and tied into compact roast, covered with fat and fell.

Leg of Lamb-Boneless
Boneless Lamb Leg

(Roast)

Lamb Leg Short Cut Sirloin Off

Leg remaining after three or four Sirloin Chops have been cut from leg. Hip bone removed, shank remaining. Some connective tissue covered by fat and fell.

Leg, Sirloin Off

(Roast)

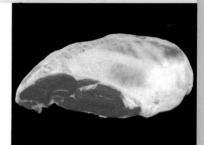

Lamb Leg Shank Half

Sirloin half removed. Lower half of leg and round leg bone included. Heavily muscled with fat and fell covering.

Shank Half Leg of Lamb
Leg-o-Lamb Shank Half

(Roast)

Lamb Leg Frenched Style Roast

Sirloin section of whole leg removed. Small amount of meat trimmed to expose 1 inch or more of shank bone.

Frenched Lamb Leg

(Roast)

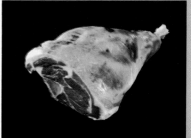

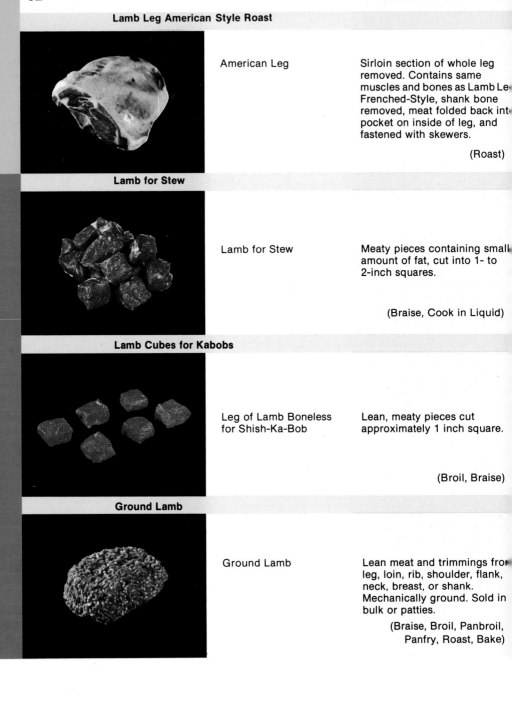

Lamb Leg American Style Roast

American Leg

Sirloin section of whole leg removed. Contains same muscles and bones as Lamb Leg Frenched-Style, shank bone removed, meat folded back into pocket on inside of leg, and fastened with skewers.

(Roast)

Lamb for Stew

Lamb for Stew

Meaty pieces containing small amount of fat, cut into 1- to 2-inch squares.

(Braise, Cook in Liquid)

Lamb Cubes for Kabobs

Leg of Lamb Boneless for Shish-Ka-Bob

Lean, meaty pieces cut approximately 1 inch square.

(Broil, Braise)

Ground Lamb

Ground Lamb

Lean meat and trimmings from leg, loin, rib, shoulder, flank, neck, breast, or shank. Mechanically ground. Sold in bulk or patties.

(Braise, Broil, Panbroil, Panfry, Roast, Bake)

Variety Meats

Once you are familiar with the many kinds of variety meats, you can take advantage of the excellent buys they offer. By choosing liver, brains, heart, kidneys, sweetbreads, tongue or tripe, you can add a great many interesting menu variations to meal planning.

There is an added advantage in using variety meats because they are economical. Most of them are in less demand than other kinds of meat and therefore are lower in price. Variety meats are also an excellent source of many essential nutrients, including protein, B vitamins, iron and

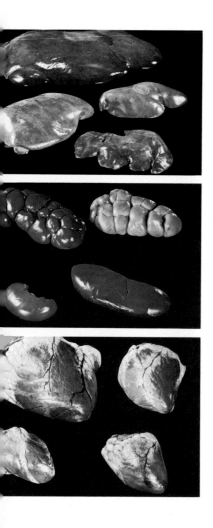

161. Livers
Pictured at top is beef. Middle left is veal. Middle right is lamb. Bottom is pork. Beef, lamb, and veal livers have two lobes, one predominantly larger than the other. Pork liver has three lobes about equal in size.

162. Kidneys
Pictured at top left is beef. Top right is veal. Lower left is lamb. Lower right is pork. Beef and veal kidneys are made up of many lobes. Pork kidney is larger than lamb kidney.

163. Hearts
Pictured in order of size: beef, veal, pork, and lamb. All are basically shaped the same. Generally sold cut or split. Beef heart has more fat than the others.

phosphorus. Liver, in particular, is a leading source of iron and vitamin A.

In the same way that many retail cuts of meat are similar to each other, variety meats from beef, veal, pork, and lamb are also similar to each other. The major difference between variety meats from different animals is size, although of course there is also some variation in flavor. Variety meats from beef are the largest; those from lamb are the smallest. The size of variety meats from veal and pork are in between beef and lamb.

164.   Tongues

Pictured in order of size: beef, veal, pork, and lamb. Rough skin covers muscles of tongue, including base. It is removed before serving. Sold fresh, cured, or cured and smoked.

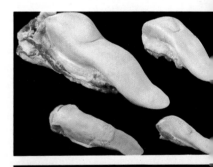

165.   Brains

All brains are a soft consistency and are covered with a thin membrane.

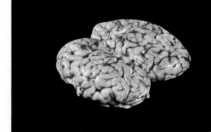

166.   Sweetbreads

Thymus glands. Creamy white, soft consistency, covered with a thin membrane. Largest from young beef, smallest from lamb. Not found in mature beef.

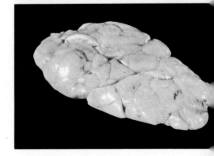

Sausages and Luncheon Meat

Sausage, one of the oldest forms of processed food, was a staple food over a thousand years before Christ. The word sausage comes from the Latin word "salsus" which means salted, or literally, preserved. By the Middle Ages sausage making had become an art that was practiced commercially by people all over Europe. Certain "wurstmachers" became so adept at spicing and processing distinctive sausages that their products became world-famous. Eventually certain sausages came to be known by the names of the towns from which they originated: Frankfurt (Germany); Bologna (Italy); Genoa (Italy); Göteberg (Sweden); and Arles (France) are some of the best-known.

There is evidence to indicate that American Indians combined chopped dried meat with dried berries to make a primitive form of dried sausage. Later, settlers arriving in America from Europe brought a tradition of fine sausage-making with them and began what was eventually to become the sausage industry of the United States.

There are more than two hundred different varieties of sausage and luncheon meat sold today, and they account for approximately 15 percent of all the red meat eaten. Approximately five billion pounds of sausage are made annually by the four thousand processors of sausage in the United States. Sausages are made from minced or ground meat, seasoned in a variety of ways and then stuffed into an edible natural fat-free animal casing or synthetic cellulose. Parafined cloth is also used as a casing for some sausage. Sometimes these products are made from all pork or all beef; more often they are a combination of several different kinds of meat and spices.

Fresh sausage always must be cooked before it can be eaten. Smoked sausage must be cooked unless it is labeled "cooked" or "fully cooked," in which case it does not have to be cooked again although flavor often is improved when it is heated. Frankfurters are a good example of fully cooked sausage that can be eaten safely without cooking. but which often are preferred heated. Ready-to-serve sausages and luncheon meat usually are sliced and served cold and may be eaten safely without further cooking.

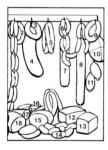

1. Austrian Sausage
2. Kiska
3. Ring Bologna
4. Beerwurst
5. Smoked Polish Sausage
6. Natural Casing Frankfurters
7. Salami
8. Large Bologna
9. Kiska
10. Minced Ham
11. Prasky
12. Peppered Loaf
13. Pickle & Pimiento Loaf
14. Knackwurst
15. Hamburger Loaf
16. Skinless Wieners
17. Liver Sausage
18. Head Cheese

3

Bulk Buying, Food Plans, and Cooperatives

There certainly is more than one way to purchase meat. If money is no object, it is possible to pick up a telephone, order meat, and have it delivered quickly—wrapped and tied with a fancy bill attached. But few people can afford this kind of luxury. Most of us are interested in finding the most economical way to buy meat without compromising the quality.

There are those who claim that buying a whole carcass, at what they believe to be wholesale prices, is a big money-saver. Others subscribe to food plans that seem to provide meat and other food at substantial discounts. Many people join food co-operatives, while others watch newspapers for supermarket specials. An analysis of all these methods will help you evaluate the differences between them and determine which method is best.

Should You Consider Buying Meat in Bulk?

Is it economical to buy meat in bulk? The answer may be "yes," but all too often, the answer probably is "no!"

In spite of the questionable economics of bulk buying, there are certain instances when it may make sense. The prime consideration should be that you know exactly what you are buying. If you live a long distance from retail stores, and you have adequate storage facilities, the savings in time and gas may make bulk purchasing worthwhile. If you simply don't have time to market regularly, the convenience of having a freezer full of meat may outweigh any disadvantages. And finally, if you have a reliable wholesale dealer who can provide meat you consider superior to the meat available at retail, there is no reason not to buy directly from him, as long as you recognize that, in most instances, you probably are not getting a bargain.

The Traps and Pitfalls of Bulk Buying

Thumbing through the evening paper you come upon a marvelously tempting advertisement offering a side of beef for an incredibly low price and just thinking about it makes your mouth water. Maybe it's been a long time since you've had steak as often as you would like. In addition to the bargain price for beef, the advertisement goes on to offer a free turkey to new customers or bonus bargains of chicken and bacon at well below retail prices. While you're considering it, it occurs to you that buying meat in quantity might be a hedge against inflation if meat prices go up. And, of course, you never can tell when meat might be in short supply, in which case it would be wonderful if you were to have a freezer full of meat. All in all it seems like a great idea.

Think again! Many wholesale dealers are reliable and honest. But unfortunately there are some dealers who are not. Therefore the first question you must ask yourself is whether the advertisement is a legitimate one, or a come-on. If the meat is advertised at a surprisingly low price, it is probable the quality of meat being offered is poor. But by the time you know that, you will be in an office talking to a super-salesman who expects you to turn down the advertised meat. He'll be more than ready to talk you into buying more expensive meat—which he will assure you is still a phenomenal buy. As a matter of fact, this kind of salesman usually has no intention of allowing you to buy the advertised meat. If *you* don't find it unacceptable, *he* will explain why the meat is inferior. Most such salesmen are quite prepared to be insulting if you insist on buying the advertised special. This sales technique is called "bait and switch." The advertisement for low-cost meat is the "bait." The salesman's effort to persuade you to buy more expensive meat is the "switch."

Since it is of vital importance that you know as much as possible about any company you contemplate dealing with, it's a good idea to check with your local Better Business Bureau or Chamber of Commerce before you invest several hundred dollars in meat, or if you suspect a "bait and switch" operation.

The Hidden Expenses

Another clue to the possibility that a dealer is not as forthright as he may appear is if he keeps extra expenses hidden. Find out if there is an extra charge for the recommended fast or "flash" freezing, which is the best method of freezing large quantities of meat because it causes the least damage to meat fibers. Is there an additional charge for cutting or properly wrapping the meat? It is generally most convenient to have ground beef wrapped in one-pound packages. Will the dealer insist on wrapping it in three-pound packages, unless you are willing to pay extra? Find out if the quoted price includes marking each package with the cut, weight, and date, so you don't end up with mysterious unidentifiable bundles in your freezer. Be sure your name is written or stenciled on every package of meat, so you can be absolutely certain you take home the same meat you saw being wrapped. And find out if the ground beef will be ground more than once without extra charge.

All these services cost the dealer money. Since he must make a profit to stay in business, it's perfectly proper for him to charge a fair amount to cover them. Sometimes these costs are already included in the advertised price. Ask, rather than assume they are included. A reliable dealer will tell you if they have been included, *before* you sign a purchase contract, rather than spring them on you at the last minute. Whether charged separately or added to the quoted price, fifteen to twenty cents per pound is fairly usual for cutting, wrapping, marking, and quick-freezing. When such costs are not included in the advertised price, it's up to you to decide whether you are still getting a bargain if you must spend another fifteen or twenty cents per pound.

How Much to Buy?

Once you have found a reliable dealer and are ready to purchase meat, the next step is to decide whether to buy a whole carcass, a side (or half) of a carcass, or a quarter. On the average, you'll need one cubic foot of freezer space to accommodate thirty-five to forty pounds of wrapped, cut meat. If the meat is packaged in odd shapes, or if the cuts have a high percentage of bone, you will need slightly more space. In the event you cannot store all the meat in your own freezer, you may be able to rent a freezer locker through the dealer or leave some of the meat with him to be picked up as you need it. If the dealer agrees to store a portion of your meat, find out if there are special restricted times for pick-ups. A dealer may require several days notice for pick-ups, and then permit them only a few days a week, at times that may be very inconvenient for many customers. If there is a charge for storage, and there may well be, you must add that expense when you estimate the cost per pound of your purchase.

If you decide to buy an entire side of beef, be absolutely certain you get both a hindquarter and a forequarter, not two hindquarters or two forequarters. Choose a quarter of a carcass instead of a side, if you prefer to buy a more limited amount of beef. The table that follows should help you to determine whether you want a hindquarter or a forequarter. Your decision will depend on the cuts of beef your family prefers and, to some extent, on your budget. A forequarter will weigh slightly more than a hindquarter, but it should also cost less per pound. In general, dealers who advertise special buys, which they call "beef bundle" or "steak package" or some other fanciful name, are trying to unload a collection of unspecific cuts which are likely to be a poor buy. Check the chapter on storage and freezing to be certain you don't buy a larger quantity of meat than you can use within the time recommended for safe storage.

APPROXIMATE YIELD OF CUTS FROM A BEEF QUARTER
(300-Pound Side, Yield Grade 3)

		% of Quarter	Pounds
Hindquarter (144 lbs.)	Round Steak	18.8%	27.0
	Rump Roast (Boneless)	6.9%	9.9
	Porterhouse, T-Bone, Club Steaks	10.6%	15.3
	Sirloin Steak	17.3%	24.9
	Flank Steak	1.0%	1.5
	Lean Trim	14.6%	21.0
	Kidney	.6%	.9
	Waste (fat, bone, and shrinkage)	30.2%	43.5
	Total Hindquarter	100.0%	144.0
Forequarter (156 lbs.)	Rib Roast (7" cut)	11.7%	18.3
	Blade Chuck Roast	17.1%	26.7
	Arm Chuck Roast (Boneless)	11.2%	17.4
	Brisket (Boneless)	4.0%	6.3
	Lean Trim	31.6%	49.2
	Waste (fat, bone, and shrinkage)	24.4%	38.1
	Total Forequarter	100.0%	156.0

The Importance of Yield Grade

In order to be certain you are buying the quality grade you want, it is important to look for the quality grade stamp on the meat you have selected. When you buy a whole carcass, a side, or a quarter, it is equally important to look for a yield or cutability grade stamp to find out how much usable meat will remain after cutting and trimming. Yield grade is not an important concern when you buy retail cuts, because you can see precisely how much meat you are buying simply by looking at the weight marked on the package. But yield is of vital importance to anyone buying a carcass or wholesale cut. Look for the yield grade carefully. It's stamped only once on each quarter; it is not rolled the length of the carcass as the quality grade stamp is.

Yield Grade	Percentage of Usable Meat from Carcass
1	82.0%
2	77.5%
3	73.0%
4	68.0%
5	63.5%

Yield grades are numbered one to five. Grade one indicates the highest or greatest yield of usable meat from a carcass. A carcass with a high yield will have minimum fat covering and very thick muscles.

The better yield grades command a slightly higher price. This is perfectly reasonable because, although two steers may weigh the same, the carcass with the better yield grade should provide a larger percentage of meat. The cost span between Yield Grade 1 and Yield Grade 5 is about six and one-half cents a pound. On a 300-pound side of beef, this amounts to about $20.

What You Are Really Buying

The price quoted per pound for a carcass, a side, or a quarter is for "hanging weight," which is the weight of the meat as it hangs on the hook, *before* bones and excess fat have been trimmed off. It is not the weight of usable meat. In other words, "hanging weight" is meat that is not trimmed at all, and it includes a great many pounds of completely unusable waste. If your bargain price is a dollar a pound, hanging weight, you're paying a dollar for every pound that goes into the garbage, too. There will be about 25 percent waste on an average side of beef. At a dollar a pound for a 300-pound side, that 75 pounds translates into at least $75.00 for absolutely nothing. The true cost of the usable meat that remains therefore rises from $1.00 to $1.33 1/3 per pound—plus a potential 15 or 20 cents a pound for freezing, cutting and wrapping.

How much of a bargain, then, is our hypothetical dollar a pound side of beef? Compared with normal retail prices for various cuts, probably not very much. A beef carcass, as a general rule, provides about one-quarter steaks, one-quarter roasts, and one-quarter stew meat and ground beef—in addition to the one-quarter waste. Only a small percentage of the steaks and roasts will come from the loin; most will be chuck and round. For the 40 or so pounds of loin you take home, the adjusted price per pound may, indeed, still be a bargain. But don't overlook the fact that you're paying the same price per pound for those 75 pounds of stew meat and ground beef.

A Few Final Words of Caution

Before you make a final decision about whether or not to buy beef in bulk, consider the cost of running a freezer. Consumer groups and suppliers of energy agree that the cost can run $50 a year or more. And, of course, this cost is in addition to the expense involved in buying a freezer. If you don't own a freezer already and must buy one, compare prices carefully. Some meat dealers offer to sell freezers to customers who purchase meat from them, and although it is possible to get a freezer for a fair price from a meat dealer, it is more likely you can get a better price at a discount house or through an appliance store. If you are not able to pay for the freezer in full at the time of purchase, but must pay for it in installments, the interest charges you will have to pay will increase the cost of the freezer.

Since it costs several hundred dollars to buy a side of beef, you may also find it necessary to pay for your meat in installments. This usually means the meat dealer will turn your account over to a finance company which will charge you a substantial amount of interest—an expense to be added to the final price of your meat. Moreover, as a third party to the transaction, the finance company will have only one concern—collecting money from you once a month. It will not be the least bit interested in whether the meat you have purchased is satisfactory.

Reliable dealers will allow you to be present when your meat is cut, so there can be no question about whether or not you are getting the carcass you have chosen. They will also package the meat in front of you and mark each package with your name. If you are present during the cutting and wrapping, you should be able to request the lean-fat ratio you want for ground beef. Although naturally you will have no control over the amount of fat that is actually part of the meat being ground, you can make sure that an undue amount of extra fat is not added during grinding.

When the transaction has been completed, some dealers ask their customers to sign a variety of documents. You should read them carefully before you sign. A reliable dealer will give you a sales document showing hanging weight, number of cuts made from the carcass, weight of each cut, quality grade, yield grade, and final price paid. Don't sign any document that contains the following type of statement:

"I have received listed merchandise in good condition."

"This is the order I selected and agree to buy."

"I accept the weight, price, primal cuts, and grade shown on the scale."

"The choice of meat was my own decision and I accept it as listed."

If you sign any of these statements you will have no legal recourse if the meat does not turn out to be what you expected or were promised.

Once you have all the information you need about a bulk purchase, compare your final cost with the cost of buying the same meat on sale at the supermarket. You may be amazed to discover that supermarket sales are often a more economical way to buy meat.

Pitfalls of Food Plans

There are a great many different kinds of food plans available and, as with companies that sell meat in bulk, there undoubtedly are honest food plans to be found—but not many. The only real advantage of a reliable food plan is that it can save time and eliminate some of the drudgery of shopping. But rarely, if ever, does a food plan really save a customer money.

To begin with, many food plans charge a membership fee. Since this fee can run as high as several hundred dollars, you'll need a substantial reduction in food prices to equal the fee, particularly if it is a yearly expense. In addition, many food plans are combination deals that involve the purchase of a freezer along with the food. In many cases, the cost of the freezer is well above what the same freezer would cost if purchased directly from a discount house or appliance store. And if the freezer is purchased on an installment plan, the interest charges can be considerable. On the other hand, if you already own a freezer, you may be charged more for food than the customer willing to buy a freezer, a fact you might have difficulty establishing.

Most food plans are sold by salesmen who visit you at home. This can create a particularly difficult situation, if you are confronted with a stubborn salesman who has no intention of leaving until he gets your signature on a contract. Fortunately, you have the legal right to cancel the contract by registered mail within three days if you have second thoughts.

Salesmen for food plans have superb training in aggressive selling, but usually haven't got the foggiest notion what kind of meat their company offers. More often than not they don't know one grade of meat from another, nor do they know the differences between various cuts of meat. What they seem to know best is fancy mathematics. The usual approach is to ask what you spend for food each week and then try to convince you their plan can supply an equal amount of food, plus a freezer, for less money.

There are several catches. It is a rare food plan that supplies *everything*. Chances are you will still have to spend money for paper products, cleaning supplies, bakery products, dairy products, carbonated beverages, fresh produce, and special food for company. Furthermore, the food rarely lasts as long as the salesman estimates. All too frequently the customer runs out of food ahead of schedule, but must continue to make monthly payments for food the family has already eaten. Since the primary concern of this book is meat, it should be pointed out that there is always the dreadful possibility you will discover that only ground beef and frankfurters are left in the freezer on the very night you invite the boss to dinner.

Some food plans assign a point value to meat, instead of a dollar value. Under this system you are charged a specific amount of money for which you receive "x" number of points worth of meat. If you don't want a particular kind of meat on the food plan list, the company will offer to substitute another meat to which they have arbitrarily assigned a similar point value. This is a particularly effective way to prevent you from having any idea of the dollar value of the meat you are buying, and it allows the company to make substitutions that are not necessarily equal in dollar value.

A quick look at the descriptions of meat offered by one food plan should raise a great many questions:

- "We guarantee that all meat is graded USDA Prime or Choice." Which are they going to supply? Prime or Choice? There is a difference in price between these grades, but the company certainly is not promising that *any* of the meat will be Prime.

- "Juicy Chuck Steaks." What kind of steaks are they going to supply? They could be Arm Steaks, Shoulder Steaks, 7-Bone Steaks, Top Blade Steaks, Eye Steaks. Will they *boneless* or *bone-in*?

- "London Broil." This could mean they are planning to supply Chuck, Plate, Flank or Round. These cuts are not equal in value.

- "Delicious Oven Roasts." This is a meaningless description that allows the company to supply almost any cut of meat — from the most expensive to the cheapest.

- "Ground Beef." There is no indication of the lean to fat ratio of the meat they are going to supply, nor is there any indication of the primal cut. The ground beef could be anything from 70 percent to 85 percent lean.

If you decide the benefits of a food plan outweigh the possible disadvantages, find a company that is open and honest about what it sells, that does not pretend to be selling food at wholesale prices, and that does not include gimmicks in its sales pitch.

Food Co-ops

Food co-ops are springing up all over the country and are a superb way to stretch food dollars. Their effectiveness has been well-documented. Many people who have not been able to locate a food co-op in their area have gotten together with a small group of friends and neighbors to form their own. The ability of a food co-op to purchase food at wholesale prices can provide tremendous savings in the overall cost of most food. Unfortunately, meat is the most difficult food for a small co-op to provide.

If a meat dealer is willing to sell to a co-op at wholesale prices, he usually will expect to sell a large piece of meat that has not been cut and packaged. Unless one member of the co-op is a professional meat cutter, this can create a serious problem. Even if the dealer is willing to cut the meat, he is not likely to provide an assortment of packages, each a different cut, weight, and grade. Few small co-ops have the facilities to store meat, nor do they have the facilities to repackage meat. Unless everyone in the group is willing to have ground beef one week and lamb chops the next week, it is almost impossible for a small co-op to purchase meat at a low enough price to make the effort and inconvenience worthwhile.

It may be possible, however, for even the smallest co-op to purchase such items as canned or unsliced processed meat, sausages, and bacon at wholesale prices. Large co-ops often are able to offer a substantial variety of meat and, in most instances, provide an economical way to market.

Watch Newspapers for Supermarket Specials

Once you have checked the cost of buying meat in bulk, through food plans, and from co-ops, check the cost of meat offered at sale prices every week in local supermarkets. Most newspapers carry advertisements from several stores, providing an easy way for you to do comparison shopping at home. If you are able to take advantage of competition between stores and buy meat when it is on sale, you may find that a supermarket is the most economical place to buy meat.

4

Storage of Meat

Our grandmothers used to go to the market every day to buy a few eggs, a quarter of a pound of butter, and just enough meat for dinner. Now, in the age of the refrigerator, most people market once or twice a week, and sometimes not even as often as that. With meat normally on the menu more than once or twice a week, procedures for safe and proper storage have become very important. It's not adequate simply to open the door of a refrigerator or freezer and put the meat inside. Meat is highly perishable and must be wrapped properly, stored at safe temperatures, and used within a specified period of time. The health and well-being of everyone who eats meat is dependent on safe storage.

How To Keep Meat in the Refrigerator

Meat should be stored in the coldest part of a refrigerator. Use a refrigerator thermometer to locate the best spot. Most modern refrigerators have special compartments for the storage of meat. These compartments are useful because they keep meat juices from dripping on other food. Advertisements frequently imply that meat keepers are actually colder than other parts of the refrigerator, but unfortunately, this is not always true. If your refrigerator has a meat keeper, check the temperature in it to determine if it really is the coldest spot.

Don't try to cram an excessive amount of meat into a meat keeper. It is important to maintain free circulation of air around packages of meat, no matter where they are stored. Prepackaged meat should be stored in the refrigerator in its original wrapping, provided it is going to be used within the time recommended for safe storage. If meat has not been prepackaged, remove the market wrapping paper and rewrap the meat loosely in waxed paper or aluminum foil in order to keep it from drying out. Meat should never be washed before it is wrapped and placed in the refrigerator. Excessive moisture encourages the growth of bacteria. As a matter of fact, most meat should not be washed before cooking either. You may wipe it with a damp towel just before cooking. If it is necessary to remove bone dust before cooking, scrape the cut surface of the meat lightly with a dull knife.

A word of caution about storing meat in a refrigerator: the ice cube compartment is not an adequate substitute for a freezer or a freezer compartment because it is not cold enough for lengthy storage. If it is necessary in an emergency to use the ice cube compartment to store meat, it should not be kept there more than a week.

If meat is not going to be used within a few days, it should be frozen rather than stored in the refrigerator. Follow the recommendations on the Storage Time Chart to be certain you don't store meat in the refrigerator longer than you should.

REFRIGERATOR STORAGE TIME
Maximum Storage Recommendations
for Fresh, Cooked, and Processed Meat

Meat	Refrigerator (36° to 40° F.)*
Beef (fresh)	2 to 4 days
Veal (fresh)	2 to 4 days
Pork (fresh)	2 to 4 days
Lamb (fresh)	2 to 4 days
Ground beef, veal, and lamb	1 to 2 days
Ground pork	1 to 2 days
Variety meats	1 to 2 days
Luncheon meats	1 week
Sausage, fresh pork	1 week
Sausage, smoked	3 to 7 days
Sausage, dry and semi-dry (unsliced)	2 to 3 weeks
Frankfurters	4 to 5 days
Bacon	5 to 7 days
Smoked ham, whole	1 week
Ham slices	3 to 4 days
Beef, corned	1 week
Leftover cooked meat	4 to 5 days

(The range in time reflects storage recommendations from several authorities. Top quality, fresh meat should be used within 2 or 3 days. Ground meat and variety meats should be used within 24 hours.)

Cured meat, cured-and-smoked meat, sausage, and ready-to-serve meat should be kept in their original wrappings and stored in the refrigerator rather than in the freezer. Luncheon meat should always be stored in the refrigerator and never frozen. Canned hams, picnics, and other perishable canned meat should also be stored in the refrigerator, unless the instructions on the can specifically state that no refrigeration is necessary.

Leftover cooked meat should be cooled, then covered or wrapped, and stored in the coldest part of the refrigerator if it is going to be used within two to four days. Otherwise it should be properly wrapped and frozen. If leftover meat is to be sliced, cubed, or ground, you will reduce the possibility of having the meat dry out by storing it uncut, and cutting it just before you use it. Meat that has been cooked in liquid may be stored in the liquid in which it was cooked. It should be cooled for at least an hour and a half, and then covered before it is placed in the refrigerator.

Meat placed in a refrigerator to defrost will keep for a few days. But it should be used as soon as possible after it has thawed. Leave the wrapping on the meat and place it on a plate to keep the juices from leaking all over the refrigerator.

How to Freeze Meat

Meat should be frozen while it's fresh and in top condition. Proper freezing of meat does not harm its flavor or tenderness; but it doesn't improve the meat either. Meat will not be any better when it is removed from the freezer than it was when it was placed there.

Prepare meat for freezing by trimming off excess fat and removing bones, when practical, to conserve freezer space. (Don't forget to use the bones in the stock pot!) Don't salt meat before freezing. Salt shortens the length of time meat can be kept safely frozen, brings moisture to the surface of the meat, and makes the meat less juicy. Divide the meat and wrap it in packages containing quantities convenient to use. When you wrap chops or meat patties together, slip a double piece of freezer wrap between the pieces of meat for easy separation during thawing.

Choose a moisture- and vapor-proof wrapping that will seal air out and lock moisture in. If air penetrates a package, moisture is drawn from the surface of the meat and the condition known as "freezer burn" develops. You can wrap meat

properly in aluminum foil, heavy-duty transparent poly-
ethylene, heavy-duty plastic bags, or specially coated freezer
paper. Freezer containers may also be used when the size of
the container fits the size of the meat. Wrap meat tightly,
pressing as much air out of the package as possible. One of
the most satisfactory methods of wrapping is the "drug store
wrap" shown in the illustration.

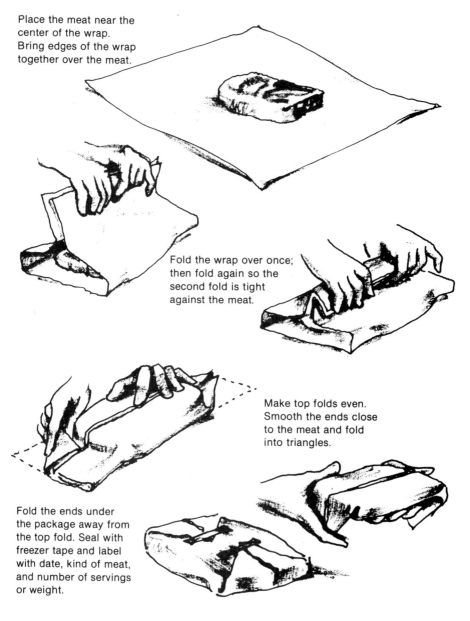

Place the meat near the center of the wrap. Bring edges of the wrap together over the meat.

Fold the wrap over once; then fold again so the second fold is tight against the meat.

Make top folds even. Smooth the ends close to the meat and fold into triangles.

Fold the ends under the package away from the top fold. Seal with freezer tape and label with date, kind of meat, and number of servings or weight.

Seal the package with freezer tape and label it, indicating the kind of meat, weight (or number of pieces or servings), and the date the meat is placed in the freezer. Use a moisture-proof marking pencil to be sure the information written on the package won't rub off. You will avoid the frustration of finding a mysterious, illegibly smudged package in your freezer at some future date.

Freeze the meat immediately at *minus* 10° F, or lower, if possible. Place it in the freezer leaving air space between the packages during initial freezing. Try to avoid freezing a large quantity of meat at one time. The temperature inside an overloaded freezer rises. Once the meat has been frozen, maintain a temperature of 0° F, or lower at all times. Higher temperatures and fluctuations of temperature above 0° F impair the quality of meat.

Use meat within the time recommended on the Storage Time Chart. Meat stored longer than the recommended time will not be top quality.

FREEZER STORAGE TIME

Maximum Storage Recommendations
for Fresh, Cooked, and Processed Meat

Meat	Freezer (at 0° F. or lower)
Beef (fresh)	6 to 12 months
Veal (fresh)	6 to 9 months
Pork (fresh)	3 to 6 months
Lamb (fresh)	6 to 9 months
Ground beef, veal, and lamb	3 to 4 months
Ground pork	1 to 3 months
Variety meats	3 to 4 months
Luncheon meats	not recommended
Sausage, fresh pork	60 days
Frankfurters	1 month
Bacon	1 month
Smoked ham, whole	60 days
Ham slices	60 days
Beef, corned	2 weeks
Leftover cooked meat	2 to 3 months

Frozen Combination Foods

Meat pies (cooked)	3 months
Swiss steak (cooked)	3 months
Stews (cooked)	3 to 4 months
Prepared meat dinners	2 to 6 months

There is a wide selection of attractive freezer-to-oven-to-table casserole dishes, which may be used to freeze cooked food. But if you leave a casserole dish in the freezer, it will not be available to use again until you thaw and heat the food stored in it. A better idea is to line the casserole dish with aluminum foil, leaving a generous overlap. Place the food in the lined dish, cover, and place in the freezer. When the food is solidly frozen, lift it out of the dish in the aluminum foil, overwrap carefully, date and mark the package, and return the wrapped food to the freezer. When you are ready to cook the food, it can be unwrapped and slipped back into the dish in which it was frozen. It will fit perfectly.

Prepackaged fresh meat may be frozen and stored in the freezer for one or two weeks without rewrapping. Just be sure there are no tears in the wrapping that would allow air to penetrate.

Frozen meat should be used on a "first in—first out" basis. In order to keep track of meat in a freezer, and to know how long each package of meat has been there, it's a good idea to tack a chart on the door of the freezer. List all of the meat stored inside, along with a notation indicating the date it was put in the freezer. Each time you use some meat, you can check it off the list. The chart can serve as a marvelous inventory of the meat you have on hand. If other members of the family help with cooking, particularly when you are not at home, you can use the chart to inform the family which meat is available for immediate use and which meat is being saved for a special occasion.

Once meat has been defrosted, it is better not to refreeze it. In an emergency it is possible to refreeze meat that is still cold, but the quality of the meat will be affected and it will be less juicy.

Refrigerators and Freezers

It's almost impossible to buy a refrigerator today that doesn't have a freezer across the top, across the bottom, or down the side. Even if you already own a full-size freezer, the chances are you also have an additional small freezer in your refrigerator, whether or not you really need it or even want it.

When you buy a new refrigerator, the size you choose should depend on the size of your family, how often you market and entertain, and the ratio of refrigerator space to freezer space you need. Refrigerators and freezers are measured by cubic feet, presumably the number of cubic feet available inside for the storage of food. But the actual cubic feet available for food storage inside most refrigerators and freezers often is less than the space advertised. Manufacturers measure "net refrigerated volume" and don't publicly take into account space taken up by shelves, trays, controls, and lights, as well as space lost around meat keepers and crispers. This loss can amount to as much as four and one-half cubic feet in a refrigerator and more than two cubic feet in a freezer.

After you have determined what size refrigerator or freezer to buy, you will be faced with the need to decide whether to buy one that must be defrosted manually or one that defrosts automatically. A chest model freezer that is defrosted manually is the least expensive freezer to operate. But almost the only other advantage to the chest model is that it loses the least amount of cold air when opened. It's very difficult to reach food at the bottom, and it's equally difficult to keep track of food once it is put into a chest model. This can be a serious problem, since food should be dated when it is stored and used within a specified amount of time. A manually-defrosted upright freezer provides a good combination of convenience and energy conservation, and you will be less likely to lose track of a tenderloin bought on sale. Freezers that are not overloaded and are not opened unnecessarily should need defrosting only about twice a year.

Refrigerators present a different problem since they are likely to be opened a great many times a day. Manually-defrosted refrigerators are supposed to cost slightly less to run because they use less electricity on a day-to-day basis than automatic defrosting models. However, in order to defrost a refrigerator manually, all the food must be removed, including the food in the freezer compartment. A considerable amount of electricity is required to bring the temperature of the refrigerator and freezer compartments back down to a safe level and to rechill food removed during defrosting.

In addition, frost builds up in a refrigerator each time the door is opened. As the frost builds up, more energy is required to run the refrigerator. As a consumer, you are more or less "damned if you do" and "damned if you don't." Either you use extra energy to rechill the refrigerator and the food if you defrost regularly, or extra energy to run the refrigerator if you permit frost to accumulate on the coils.

If you buy a no-frost refrigerator you certainly will save yourself a great deal of work. Your energy consumption will be just about the same as it would be with a manually defrosted refrigerator. There's an added bonus: meat is better when it is kept at a constant temperature. The flavor and texture are not helped when meat is removed from a refrigerator or freezer compartment during frequent defrosting.

Refrigerator-freezer combinations usually have separate temperature controls for each compartment. Any appliance that does not have separate controls is a poor buy. The refrigerator should be kept between 36° F and 40° F. The freezer should be kept at 0° F to minus 10° F, or lower. Sometimes the settings on the separate controls affect each other, and it may be necessary to juggle them a bit in order to find the proper settings for each compartment. If you want to find out whether your equipment is maintaining a steady, reliable, safe temperature, it's a good idea to use a freezer/refrigerator thermometer. One particularly helpful thermometer that is available can be read from the outside, allowing you to tell at a glance what the temperature is inside, without opening a door and allowing cold air to escape. This is especially helpful in the event of a power failure because you can monitor the temperature easily during the time you should avoid opening the refrigerator or freezer door. By keeping track of how high the temperature gets in a freezer or refrigerator during a power failure, you will be able to determine if the food inside must be thrown away, should be cooked immediately, or may safely be left inside to use when you normally would use it. Of course, if there is a power failure, you may need a flashlight or candle to read the thermometer!

5

Basic Cooking Information

You'll find that the best recipe for success in the kitchen is a combination of the right ingredients and the correct cooking method. No dish can be better than the basic ingredients put into it, but even the use of the best ingredients won't guarantee a good dinner if the food is not cooked properly. Fortunately choosing the best meat does *not* mean buying the most expensive meat. But it does mean selecting the correct or most suitable cut of meat for a recipe and for the planned method of cooking. Since it is important that all the ingredients used in a recipe be of good quality, choose a recipe that does not call for a long list of expensive ingredients if economy is important. It is much better, for example, to braise meat in a good simple stock than in a poor-quality wine.

A successful meal depends on reliable recipes, careful planning, proper ingredients, a knowledge of correct cooking methods, the right equipment, good organization, and accurate timing. Appreciative, hungry diners help too. But more than anything else, you need imagination and the courage to experiment.

A Good Basic Cookbook Is as Helpful as a Good Dictionary

There are more books published and sold each year on the subject of cooking than on almost any other subject. And it isn't always easy to know which books to buy. A cookbook often seems appealing because it has mouth-watering photographs, but good pictures are not a guarantee of reliable recipes. You need to develop a set of standards for what you expect from a cookbook, and then choose one that meets the criteria you have set.

A worthwhile cookbook collection should begin with a basic cookbook. There are a few very good standard books that have been available for several years, and they are updated periodically. These are not necessarily glamorous books; but they are filled with vital information many readers never discover. Instead of using a basic book just for a few specific recipes, look for sections on cooking methods, equivalents, substitutions, definitions, weights and measures, nutrition, special diets, and a great many other subjects. Cooking teachers are often surprised and distressed at how many basic questions they are asked, many of which are fully answered in books their students own. There is no need to memorize an endless collection of facts if you don't want to, when it is so easy to own a cookbook that contains the information you need. But in order to find this information, you have to learn to look for it.

Once you own a basic book, you can go on to collect more specialized books—by authors you know and admire or on specific kinds of food or cooking methods that are of particular interest. There are excellent books available on ethnic cooking—French, Italian, Oriental, etc. There are also excellent books to choose from on casseroles, baking, company dishes, and just about any type of food you might want to cook. Many food manufacturers and processors have published informative books, on particular foods and special ingredients, which are well worth having. And don't overlook the helpful books and booklets (often free) that provide specific information on how to cook with specialized equipment, like slow-cookers and microwave ovens.

An Inaccurate Recipe Can Spell Disaster

The important thing to determine each time you buy a cookbook is whether the book has detailed, reliable recipes. Read a few pages before you buy a book and find out if the instructions are written simply and clearly. If the ingredients call for "a large can of tomato sauce," question what the writer means. How large is large? Cans of tomato sauce are available in a great many sizes. Make sure the instructions tell you such things as whether to cover a casserole when you bake it, whether to sift flour before you measure it, approximately how long something will take to cook, or approximately how many people a recipe will serve. You may be surprised to discover that some of the best cooks and cooking teachers don't know how to write a recipe that is clear and easy to follow. Each time you consider buying a cookbook, take time to evaluate it to decide if it is a book you will find helpful to own.

The "How To" of Cooking Meat

Two factors determine the correct way to cook meat—grade and cut. Both of these factors relate to the tenderness of meat. Essentially, this means that tender meat can be cooked one way, less tender meat must be cooked in a different way.

Most tender cuts of meat are cooked by dry heat— roasted, broiled, panbroiled, or panfried. Veal is an exception. Veal steaks or chops are tender cuts, but they don't have enough internal fat or marbling for broiling and therefore should be braised or sautéed.

Less tender cuts of meat are made tender by cooking with moist heat: surrounding the meat with steam, or cooking the meat in liquid. These cuts usually are braised. They may be browned, if desired, and then cooked in a small amount of liquid in a covered utensil. Some large cuts, such as beef brisket, and some small cuts, like stew meat, are cooked in liquid. They may also be browned, if desired, and then are completely covered by liquid and cooked in a covered utensil.

Time and Temperature

In addition to providing instructions on the correct cooking method, a good recipe will also provide information on the total cooking time required. But cooking times given in a recipe can only be approximate because there are many factors that must be taken into consideration.

- A slight variation in temperature affects the time required to cook meat, or anything else. This is particularly important when meat is cooked in an oven. Every time you open an oven door to check the progress of a roast, the temperature drops substantially and cooking time is affected. It is important to use an oven thermometer to find out if the temperature inside a closed oven remains constant and corresponds to the temperature at which it was set. It's a good idea to have an oven calibrated once a year. If you set the oven at 350° F and your oven thermometer tells you it's actually 375° F, it's vital to have a service man come and make the necessary adjustment. In the meantime, remember to take temperature deviation into account when you set the oven.

- As a general rule, a large cut of meat requires fewer minutes per pound to cook than a smaller cut. However, a chunky cut of meat needs a longer time to cook than a flat, thin cut of the same weight.

- Cuts from aged meat require slightly less cooking time than meat that has not been aged.

- No recipe, cooking timetable, or set of instructions can anticipate whether you want to serve meat rare, medium, or well-done. Use a meat thermometer to eliminate guesswork and to avoid disaster.

The temperature at which meat is cooked affects what happens to meat during cooking. The higher the temperature, the greater the shrinkage. Meat is more tender, juicy, and flavorful, and more uniformly done when cooked slowly at moderate heat than when cooked rapidly at high heat.

The Many Ways to Cook Meat

There are six basic methods for cooking meat: roasting, broiling or grilling, pan-broiling or griddle-broiling, frying (which includes pan-frying or sautéing, deep-fat frying, and stir-frying), braising, and cooking in liquid. The method you use depends on the tenderness of the meat, its size and thickness, the recipe, the cooking facilities available, and sometimes on who is coming for dinner.

Roasting   Roasting is the cooking method recommended for large tender cuts. It should be done in the following way if a standard gas or electric oven is used:

- Season meat, if desired, either before or after roasting. Seasoning, rubbed into the surface of a roast before cooking, adds to the aroma during cooking and to the flavor of the surface of the roast. Salt may be used before roasting because it will not penetrate the meat more than one-quarter to one-half an inch, although salt should not be used before cooking when meat is broiled, sautéed, or deep fried.

- Place the meat, fat side up, on a rack in a shallow roasting pan. The rack will keep the roast from sitting in melted fat and drippings, and using it will increase the circulation of heat around the meat. As the fat on the top of a roast melts, the

meat is basted naturally, eliminating the necessity for additional basting. Some cuts of meat, such as ribs of beef or
pork loin roasts, have their own natural racks formed by the
ribs. When they are cooked, the metal rack may be used or it
may be eliminated.

- *Don't* add water to the roasting pan and *don't* cover the pan. If
you do, your meat will be steamed rather than roasted.
Roasting is a dry-heat method of cooking. Water obviously
adds moisture and a cover creates steam.

- Set the oven temperature at 350° F for a small roast. Larger
roasts may be cooked at 300° F. Place meat in a preheated
oven. If you are going to use a timer to help you remember
when to check the roast, remember to set the timer when the
roast goes into the oven.

- About thirty minutes before you think the meat is cooked,
insert a meat thermometer in the roast, placing the bulb or tip
in the center of the largest muscle. The bulb should never
touch the bone or rest in fat. Position the thermometer so you
don't have to stand on your head to read it when you look in
the oven. Use the roasting timetable that follows to estimate
the amount of time required for meat to reach the internal
temperature you prefer—rare, medium, or well-done.

- Roasts are easiest to carve if they are allowed to "set" for
fifteen or twenty minutes after they have been removed from
the oven.

- Remove the roast from the oven when it reaches an internal
temperature five to ten degrees below the temperature you
want. Meat will continue to cook while it "sets" and will not
cool off too rapidly.

The Searing Method of Roasting   The myth still exists that
the searing of meat before roasting or broiling will prevent the
escape of juices during cooking. This has been proven in-
correct. Searing usually browns the surface of the meat and
helps produce exceptionally rich brown drippings. On the
other hand, seared meat has a higher degree of shrinkage,
due to fat loss, than meat that is not seared. To sear roasts
properly:

- Preheat the oven to 450° F. Prepare the roast in the standard
way.

- Place the meat in a hot oven to brown for about twenty minutes.

- Reduce the oven temperature to 250° F or 300° F by turning the regulator down and leaving the oven door open for a few minutes. Don't forget to close the oven door when the oven temperature has been reduced to the correct temperature so you can continue to cook the roast until it reaches the internal temperature desired.

Rare, Medium, or Well-Done?   Most people have very strong perferences about how they like to eat beef. Those who prefer to eat it rare usually refuse to touch a well-done hamburger or a piece of well-done steak or roast beef. On the other hand, those who insist on eating beef well-done are likely to shudder at the thought of eating it rare. Probably the largest number of people eat it cooked half way between, or medium. In most instances, a tender cut of beef may be cooked to suit individual preferences. The one possible exception is a tenderloin of beef which should be eaten rare. It is pointless to invest in an expensive tenderloin unless it is going to be served rare, because it is a particularly tender, juicy, flavorful cut of beef that turns dry and tasteless when it is overcooked.

Veal should be cooked to an internal temperature of 170° F in order to develop flavor and keep the meat tender. Fresh pork should also be cooked to an internal temperature of 170° F, although cured or cured-and-smoked pork does not have to be cooked as long.

The answer to how to cook lamb may depend on what part of the world a person comes from. In the United States, traditionally, lamb has been cooked well-done, and many Americans have never eaten lamb cooked any other way. But in most of Europe, especially France, lamb is served rare. Americans who have never particularly cared for lamb have begun to reassess their opinion as they discover lamb is more juicy and has a finer, more subtle flavor when it is served rare. As a result, more and more good restaurants in the United States are serving lamb rare, unless a customer insists on having it well-done. The trend toward eating lamb rare or medium has become so extensive that many manufacturers of meat thermometers are changing the markings on new thermometers to indicate that lamb may be served when it reaches an internal temperature of 140° F. If you have never eaten lamb cooked either rare or medium, try it. You may be surprised to discover how delicious it is, and you will certainly find it is juicier than well-done lamb.

TIMETABLE FOR ROASTING*

(300° F.-325° F. Oven Temperature)

CUT	Approx. Weight in Pounds	Meat Thermometer Reading	Approx.† Cooking Time Min. per lb.
BEEF			
Rib[1]	6 to 8	140° F. (rare)	23 to 25
		160° F. (medium)	27 to 30
		170° F. (well)	32 to 35
Rib[1]	4 to 6	140° F. (rare)	26 to 32
		160° F. (medium)	34 to 38
		170° F. (well)	40 to 42
Rib Eye[2] **(Delmonico)**	4 to 6	140° F. (rare)	18 to 20
		160° F. (medium)	20 to 22
		170° F. (well)	22 to 24
Tenderloin whole[3]	4 to 6	140° F. (rare)	45 to 60 (total)
Tenderloin half[3]	2 to 3	140° F. (rare)	45 to 50 (total)
Boneless rump (rolled) (high quality)	4 to 6	150° F.-170° F.	25 to 30
Tip (high quality)	3½ to 4	140° F.-170° F.	35 to 40
	6 to 8	140° F.-170° F.	30 to 35
Ground Beef loaf (9″ × 5″)	1½ to 2½	160° F.-170° F.	1 to 1½ hrs. (total)
VEAL			
Leg	5 to 8	170° F.	25 to 35
Loin	4 to 6	170° F.	30 to 35
Rib (rack)	3 to 5	170° F.	35 to 40
Boneless shoulder	4 to 6	170° F.	40 to 45

† **Based on meat taken directly from the refrigerator.**
[1] **Ribs which measure 6 to 7 inches from chine bone to tip of rib.**
[2] **Roast at 350° F. oven temperature.**
[3] **Roast at 425° F. oven temperature.**
* **Note: Remember, roasted meat continues to cook after it has been removed from the oven. In order to avoid overcooking, remove meat from the oven when the internal temperature is 5 to 10 degrees *below* the temperature at which meat is to be served.**

TIMETABLE FOR ROASTING*

(325° F.-350° F. Oven Temperature)

CUT		Approx. Weight in Pounds	Meat Thermometer Reading	Approx.† Cooking Time Min. per lb.
PORK FRESH	**Loin**			
	Center	3 to 5	170° F.	30 to 35
	Half	5 to 7	170° F.	35 to 40
	Blade Loin or Sirloin	3 to 4	170° F.	40 to 45
	Top (double)	3 to 5	170° F.	35 to 40
	Top	2 to 4	170° F.	30 to 35
	Crown	4 to 6	170° F.	35 to 40
	Arm Picnic Shoulder			
	Bone-in	5 to 8	170° F.	30 to 35
	Boneless	3 to 5	170° F.	35 to 40
	Cushion	3 to 5	170° F.	30 to 35
	Blade Boston Shoulder	4 to 6	170° F.	40 to 45
	Leg (fresh ham)			
	Whole (bone-in)	12 to 16	170° F.	22 to 26
	Whole (boneless)	10 to 14	170° F.	24 to 28
	Half (bone-in)	5 to 8	170° F.	35 to 40
	Tenderloin	½ to 1		45 to 60
	Back Ribs		All	**1½ to 2½ hrs.
	Country-style Ribs		cooked	**1½ to 2½ hrs.
	Spareribs		well	**1½ to 2½ hrs.
	Ground Pork Loaf	2	done	**1¾ hrs.

300° F. to 325° F. Oven Temperature

CUT		Approx. Weight in Pounds	Meat Thermometer Reading	Approx.† Cooking Time Min. per lb.
PORK SMOKED	**Ham (cook-before-eating)**			
	Whole	10 to 14	160° F.	18 to 20
	Half	5 to 7	160° F.	22 to 25
	Shank Portion	3 to 4	160° F.	35 to 40
	Rump Portion	3 to 4	160° F.	35 to 40
	Ham (fully cooked)			
	Whole	10 to 14	140° F.	15 to 18
	Half	5 to 7	140° F.	18 to 24
	Loin	3 to 5	160° F.	25 to 30
	Arm Picnic Shoulder (cook-before-eating)	5 to 8	170° F.	30 to 35
	Arm Picnic Shoulder (fully-cooked)	5 to 8	140° F.	25 to 30
	Shoulder Roll (Butt)	2 to 4	170° F.	35 to 40
	Canadian-style Bacon	2 to 4	160° F.	35 to 40
	Ham Kabobs	1 to 1½" cubes		45 to 60
	Ground Ham Loaf	2	160° F.	**1½ hrs.
	Ground Ham Patties	1" thick	160° F.	45 to 60

† **Based on meat taken directly from the refrigerator.**   **Total Time

* **Note: Remember, roasted meat continues to cook after it has been removed from the oven. In order to avoid overcooking, remove meat from the oven when the internal temperature is 5 to 10 degrees *below* the temperature at which meat is to be served.**

TIMETABLE FOR ROASTING*

(300° F.-325° F. Oven Temperature)

CUT	Approx. Weight in Pounds	Meat Thermometer Reading	Approx.† Cooking Time Min. per lb.
Leg	**5 to 9**	140° F. (rare)	20 to 25
		160° F. (medium)	25 to 30
		170° F.-180° F. (well)	30 to 35
Leg, Shank Half	**3 to 4**	140° F. (rare)	25 to 30
		160° F. (medium)	30 to 35
		170° F.-180° F. (well)	35 to 40
Leg, Sirloin Half	**3 to 4**	140° F. (rare)	20 to 25
		160° F. (medium)	25 to 30
		170° F.-180° F. (well)	30 to 35
Leg, Boneless	**4 to 7**	140° F. (rare)	25 to 30
		160° F. (medium)	30 to 35
		170° F.-180° F. (well)	35 to 40
Crown Roast	**2½ to 4**	140° F. (rare)	30 to 35
		160° F. (medium)	35 to 40
		170° F.-180° F. (well)	40 to 45
Shoulder, Square Cut	**4 to 6**	160° F. (medium)	25 to 30
		170° F.-180° F. (well)	30 to 35
Shoulder, Boneless	**3½ to 5**	140° F. (rare)	30 to 35
		160° F. (medium)	35 to 40
		170° F.-180° F. (well)	40 to 45
Shoulder, Cushion	**3½ to 5**	170° F.-180° F. (well)	30 to 35
Rib‡	**1½ to 2**	140° F. (rare)	30 to 35
		160° F. (medium)	35 to 40
		170° F.-180° F. (well)	40 to 45
Rib‡	**2 to 3**	140° F. (rare)	25 to 30
		160° F. (medium)	30 to 35
		170° F.-180° F. (well)	35 to 40

LAMB (bracket spanning all lamb cuts)

†Based on meat taken directly from the refrigerator.

‡Roast at 375° F. oven temperature.

*Note: Remember, roasted meat continues to cook after it has been removed from the oven. In order to avoid overcooking, remove meat from the oven when the internal temperature is 5 to 10 degrees *below* the temperature at which meat is to be served.

Broiling   Broiling is a suitable cooking method for tender beef steaks, lamb chops, pork chops, sliced ham, bacon, and ground beef or lamb patties. Steaks and chops should be cut at least three-quarters of an inch thick, and sliced ham should be cut at least half an inch thick. The following steps are recommended for successful broiling:

- Set the oven regulator for broiling.

- *Do not season!* (Yet.)

- Place the meat on a rack of a broiler pan two to five inches from the heat, depending on the thickness of the meat. Cuts that are only three-quarters to one inch thick should be placed two to three inches from the heat; thicker cuts should be placed three to five inches from the heat.

- Broil until the top of the meat is browned (lightly browned for cured and smoked pork). Meat should be approximately half cooked (or slightly more) by the time the top is browned.

- Season the cooked side of the meat with salt and other seasonings, if desired. (Don't add salt to ham or bacon.) It's better to add salt to broiled meat *after* the surface has been browned because salt tends to delay browning, and as a result, the meat sometimes is unintentionally overcooked.

- Turn the meat over to brown the other side.

- Season the second side if desired and serve immediately.

Use the following table as a guide to broiling times. It's a good idea to use a meat thermometer to judge the degree of doneness of thick steaks and chops, and to avoid having to guess when the meat is done. But don't leave the thermometer in the meat while it is cooking.

TIMETABLE FOR BROILING

	CUT	Approx. Thickness	Weight in Pounds	Approximate Total Cooking Time Minutes	
				Rare	Medium
BEEF	**Chuck Steak (high quality)**	1 inch	1½ to 2½	24	30
		1½ inches	2 to 4	40	45
	Rib Steak	1 inch	1 to 1½	15	20
		1½ inches	1½ to 2	25	30
		2 inches	2 to 2½	35	45
	Rib Eye Steak (Delmonico)—	1 inch	8 to 10 ozs.	15	20
		1½ inches	12 to 14 ozs.	25	30
		2 inches	16 to 20 ozs.	35	45
	Top Loin Steak	1 inch	1 to 1½	15	20
		1½ inches	1½ to 2	25	30
		2 inches	2 to 2½	35	45
	Sirloin steak	1 inch	1½ to 3	20	25
		1½ inches	2¼ to 4	30	35
		2 inches	3 to 5	40	45
	Porterhouse steak—	1 inch	1¼ to 2	20	25
		1½ inches	2 to 3	30	35
		2 inches	2½ to 3½	40	45
	Tenderloin (Filet Mignon)		4 to 8 ozs.	10 to 15	15 to 20
	Ground Beef Patties	1 inch thick by 3 inches	4 ozs.	15	25

Rare steaks are broiled to an internal temperature of 140° F.,
medium to 160° F., well-done to 170° F.

TIMETABLE FOR BROILING

CUT	Approx. Thickness	Approx. Total Cooking Time Minutes
PORK		
FRESH		
Rib or Loin Chops	¾ to 1 inch	20 to 25
Shoulder Steaks	½ to ¾ in.	20 to 22
Ground Pork Patties	1 inch	20 to 25
Pork Kabobs	1½ × 1½ × ¾ to 1 inch	22 to 25
SMOKED		
Ham Slice	½ inch	10 to 12
Ham Slice	1 inch	16 to 20
Loin Chops	½ to ¾ in.	15 to 20
Canadian-style Bacon		
Sliced	¼ inch	6 to 8
Sliced	½ inch	8 to 10
Bacon		4 to 5
Ground Ham Patties	1 inch	16 to 20

CUT	Approx. Thickness	Approx. Weight in Ounces	Approx. Total Cooking Time Minutes
LAMB			
Shoulder Chops	¾ to 1 inch	5 to 9	10 to 12
Rib Chops	1 inch	4 to 6	12
	1½ inches	6 to 8	18
	2 inches	8 to 12	22
Loin Chops	1 inch	4 to 7	12
	1½ inches	7 to 10	18
	2 inches	8 to 14	22
Sirloin Chops	¾ to 1 inch	6 to 12	12 to 14
Leg Chops (Steaks)	¾ to 1 inch	10 to 14	14 to 18
Cubes for Kabobs	1 to 1½ inches		12 to 18
	1½ to 2 inches		18 to 22
Ground lamb Patties	1 inch by 3 inches	4	18

The same tender cuts of meat suitable for broiling are also suitable for pan-broiling if they are no thicker than one inch. Pan-broiling is a convenient method for cooking a small steak or just a few chops. The following steps are recommended for successful pan-broiling: **Pan-broiling**

- Place the meat in a heavy skillet or on a griddle.

- *Don't* add water. *Don't* cover the pan. Pan-broiling is a dry heat method of cooking, and therefore no water should be added and no cover used. Adding either changes the cooking method to braising. Most cuts of meat appropriate for pan-broiling have enough natural fat to prevent them from sticking to the pan. However, if the meat is very lean, the pan may be brushed with a small amount of fat.

- Cook slowly over moderate heat, turning occasionally to brown the meat evenly on both sides. Since the surface of the meat is in constant contact with the hot surface of the pan, it's essential to turn the meat periodically to insure even cooking.

- Pour off the fat as it accumulates during cooking. If the fat is permitted to collect in the pan, the meat will be pan-fried (or sautéed) instead of being pan-broiled.

- Pan-broiling takes about half the amount of time required to broil the same cut of meat. Don't overcook. Test for doneness in a bone-in steak or chop by cutting a small gash near the bone to check the color of the cooked meat.

- Season if desired and serve immediately.

When a recipe calls for browning ground beef, many cooks make the mistake of adding fat to the pan, particularly since so many recipes call for the addition of fat. Even lean ground beef usually has enough natural fat to make additional fat unnecessary, in spite of what many recipes recommend. Pan-broiling is the correct method for browning ground beef and the fat should be poured off as it accumulates. Salt should be added after the meat has been browned.

There are two methods of frying meat: When a small amount of fat is added to the pan before the meat is added, or when fat is allowed to accumulate in the pan during cooking, the method is called pan-frying or sautéing. When meat is totally immersed in cooking oil, the technique is deep-fat frying. **Frying**

A variation of pan-frying is stir-frying. Thin strips of meat are cooked very quickly, often with vegetables, in a small amount of cooking oil over high heat, in the Oriental fashion.

Pan-frying or Sautéing Meat that is suitable for pan-frying includes comparatively thin pieces of tender meat, meat made tender by pounding, scoring, cubing, or grinding, and leftover meat. Use the following method:

- If the meat is very lean, or if the meat has been breaded or floured, add a small amount of fat to the pan and brown the meat on both sides. If uncoated meat has enough natural fat, additional fat does not have to be added to the pan, but it should be allowed to accumulate in the pan during cooking.

- If meat is coated, seasoning may be added to the coating mixture before cooking. Otherwise the meat should be seasoned after it has been browned.

- *Don't* cover the pan during cooking. If the pan is covered, the meat will be braised rather than pan-fried or sautéed, and it will not be crisp. The object of frying meat is to make it crisp and flavorful, even though sometimes tenderness may be sacrificed.

- Cook at moderate heat, turning occasionally until done. Smoking fat means it is burning, and the temperature is too high for both the fat and for the meat. The meat should be cooked through as it browns. Turn the meat occasionally to insure even cooking.

- Season uncoated meat if desired.

- Remove the cooked meat from the pan with a slotted spoon, tongs, or spatula and serve at once.

Deep-fat frying Meat that is to be deep-fried usually is coated with egg and then with seasoned bread crumbs. Or it may be dipped in a seasoned batter, or dredged in seasoned flour or cornmeal. Follow these steps for the best results:

- Use an electric deep-fryer or a deep pot, a wire frying basket, and enough cooking oil to cover the meat completely.

- Preheat the cooking oil to the correct temperature. Proper temperatures range from 300° F to 360° F, depending on the size of the pieces of meat and on whether the meat to be deep-fried is uncooked or has been precooked. It is essential to cook the meat in an automatically controlled deep-fryer or to use a special deep-fat-frying thermometer to check the temperature of the oil.

- Place only enough meat in the frying basket to cover the bottom of the basket.

- Lower the basket into the hot oil gradually.

- Cook until the meat is browned and cooked through. Since meat is surrounded by hot oil, no turning is necessary. Cooking time will be less than the time required for pan-frying.

- When the meat is cooked, drain the oil from the basket back into the pot and place the meat on paper toweling to remove excess oil. Put the cooked meat in a low oven to keep warm while the remainder of the meat is being cooked.

    If the cooking oil is properly cared for, it may be used more than once. Strain it through cheesecloth, or a clean paper coffee filter; cool, cover, and store it in the refrigerator. If the oil has picked up a strong odor from the food it was cooked in, fry a few slices of raw potato in the slightly cooled oil. The potatoes will absorb the odor. Add a small amount of new oil each time the oil is reused. Replace the oil completely if it foams or fails to brown food properly.

Stir-Frying   The technique of stir-frying is Asian and is one of the basic methods of Chinese cooking. A wok, a conical-shaped pan with deep sloping sides (or in an emergency, a large heavy skillet) is placed over high heat. A small amount of cooking oil is added to the pan. Meat should be cut into small, uniform-size pieces and cooked in hot, but not smoking, oil. It should be stirred constantly while it cooks, usually about two or three minutes. In many instances the meat is marinated before cooking, and vegetables are added to the wok during cooking. Wooden chopsticks are often used for stirring.

Tips on breading   The most successful way to bread food is to season it, dredge it in flour, shake off the excess flour, dip it in eggs seasoned and beaten with a few drops of cooking oil, shake off excess egg mixture, lay in crumbs made from fresh bread, and pat crumbs on meat.

A great many people have difficulty cooking breaded meat. If you usually end up with the breading firmly stuck to the pan instead of the meat, there are two things you can do:

- When a recipe calls for dipping meat in beaten egg mixed with water, substitute cooking oil for the water. If no water is called for in the recipe, add a teaspoon of cooking oil to the beaten egg anyway.

- After the meat has been breaded, put it between pieces of waxed paper and place it in the refrigerator for at least half an hour before cooking.

Braising The proper cooking method for less tender cuts of meat is braising. Some tender cuts of pork and veal, such as chops, steaks, and cutlets, are also braised. Braising is done in the following way:

- Add fat to a heavy utensil, unless the cut of meat has a sufficient amount of natural fat. Brown the meat slowly on all sides. Browning helps develop flavor and eye appeal. A "slow brown" stays on the meat better than a "quick brown" obtained at a high temperature.

- Remove the meat from the pan and pour off the grease. Deglaze the pan.*

- Season the meat.

- Return the meat to the cooking utensil and add a small amount of liquid. Stock, wine, water, vegetable juices, and clear soup are all suitable.

- Cover tightly.

- Cook at a low temperature until the meat is tender. Meat may be simmered on top of the range or cooked covered in a 300° F to 325° F oven. Vegetables may be added to the meat at any appropriate time during cooking, so they will be tender but not overcooked when the meat is done. Additional liquid may be added during cooking if necessary.

*Deglazing a pan is an important cooking procedure that prevents the loss of all those delicious coagulated juices or drippings that collect in a pan. It is done after the meat has been browned or roasted, so the drippings can be added to the liquid in which meat is cooked, or to a sauce or gravy. To deglaze, pour off excess fat and then add a small amount of stock, water, or wine to the pan. Use a liquid that is compatible with that used for braising or in the gravy. Dry vermouth is excellent. Scrape up the drippings over high heat, using a wooden spoon.

- Remove the meat and vegetables to a platter and keep them warm while you make a gravy or sauce. Use the drippings in the pan for the gravy.

TIMETABLE FOR BRAISING

		Approx. Weight or Thickness	Approx. Total Cooking Time
BEEF	Pot-roast	3 to 5 pounds	2½ to 3½ hours
	Short Ribs	Pieces (2 in. × 2 in. × 4 in.)	1½ to 2½ hours
	Flank Steak	1½ to 2 pounds	1½ to 2½ hours
	Stuffed Steak	½ to ¾ inch	1½ hours
	Round Steak	¾ to 1 inch	1 to 1½ hours
	Cubes	1 inch	1 to 1½ hours
		2 inches	1½ to 2½ hours
VEAL	Breast, Stuffed	3 to 4 pounds	1½ to 2½ hours
	Breast, Boneless	2 to 3 pounds	1½ to 2½ hours
	Riblets		2 to 3 hours
	Chops	½ to ¾ inch	45 to 60 minutes
	Steaks or cutlets	½ to ¾ inch	45 to 60 minutes
	Cubes	1 to 2 inches	45 to 60 minutes
PORK	Chops, Fresh	¾ to 1½ inches	45 to 60 minutes
	Spareribs	2 to 3 pounds	1½ hours
	Backribs		1½ to 2 hours
	Country-style Ribs		1½ to 2 hours
	Tenderloin		
	Whole	¾ to 1 pound	45 to 60 minutes
	Fillets	½ inch	30 minutes
	Shoulder Steaks	¾ inch	45 to 60 minutes
	Cubes	1 to 1¼ inches	45 to 60 minutes
LAMB	Neck Slices	¾ inch	1 hour
	Shoulder Chops	¾ to 1 inch	45 to 60 minutes
	Breast, Stuffed	2 to 3 pounds	1½ to 2 hours
	Breast, Rolled	1½ to 2 pounds	1½ to 2 hours
	Riblets		1½ to 2½ hours
	Shanks	¾ to 1 pound each	1 to 1½ hours
	Lamb for Stew	1½-inch cubes	1½ to 2 hours

Cooking in Liquid Large cuts of less tender meat and stews are cooked in liquid. The general procedures for cooking both are similar, although there are a few minor differences.

Large Cuts
- Brown meat on all sides if desired, using a heavy utensil and adding a small amount of fat if necessary. Don't brown corned beef or cured-and-smoked pork.

- Drain off the fat.

- Deglaze the pan.

- Season the meat as desired. Don't add salt to corned beef or to cured or smoked meat. It is already salty enough.

- Cover the meat with liquid. Meat will not have to be turned, and uniform cooking will be assured if the meat is completely covered.

- Add appropriate herbs and spices to the liquid. You may also add cut vegetables such as celery (and celery tops), green pepper, cloves of garlic, onion, scallions, or shallots, for additional flavoring.

- Cover the utensil and simmer the meat until tender, adding more liquid during cooking if necessary. Boiling or over-cooking will shrink the meat, make it dry and less flavorful, and make it difficult to slice.

- Add vegetables during cooking if desired, but don't add them too soon or they will be overcooked.

- If the meat is to be served cold, allow it to cool for at least an hour and a half in the liquid or stock in which it was cooked. Cover the meat and chill it in the refrigerator. Shrinkage will be reduced if the meat is cooled in liquid, and the meat will be juicier and more flavorful than meat that is removed from the cooking liquid immediately and then placed directly in the refrigerator.

Stews Meat should be cut into uniform-size pieces, and excess fat should be trimmed off. One and one-half inch cubes are a good size, although the meat may also be cut into rectangular shapes or long narrow strips.

- If the meat has been dredged in seasoned flour, it must be browned in a small amount of fat in a heavy skillet. If the meat has not been coated, browning is optional.

- Season the meat.

- Add just enough liquid, hot or cold, to cover the meat.

- Add appropriate herbs and spices to the liquid.

- Cover the pan and simmer until the meat is tender. Don't boil. If necessary, add additional liquid.

- Add appropriate vegetables at the proper times during cooking.

- When the meat and vegetables are cooked, remove them to a platter and keep them warm.

- Add any vegetables that may have been cooked separately.

- Thicken the liquid in which the meat was cooked to make a gravy or sauce.

TIMETABLE FOR COOKING IN LIQUID

		Approximate Weight or size	Approx. Total Cooking Time (Hours)
BEEF	Fresh or corned beef	4 to 6 pounds	3½ to 4½
	Shank Cross Cuts	¾ to 1¼ pounds	2½ to 3
	Beef for Stew		2½ to 3½
VEAL	Veal for Stew		2 to 3
PORK FRESH	Spareribs		2 to 2½
	Country-style Ribs		2 to 2½
	Hocks		2½ to 3
PORK SMOKED	Ham (old style and country-cured)		
	Large	12 to 16 pounds	4½ to 5
	Small	10 to 12 pounds	4½ to 5
	Half	5 to 8 pounds	3 to 4
	Arm Picnic Shoulder	5 to 8 pounds	3½ to 4
	Shoulder Roll	2 to 4 pounds	1½ to 2
	Hocks		2 to 2½
LAMB	Lamb for Stew	1 to 1½-inch cubes	1½ to 2

How to Make Gravy—Quickly and Simply

A smooth and delicious gravy or sauce can be made more easily than many people think. Take butter, or some of the fat in which the meat was browned, and heat it in a saucepan. When butter is used instead of fat drippings, gravy will be paler in color. Add an equal amount of flour and stir to a nut brown smooth paste over moderate heat. This mixture is called a *roux*. It will take only two or three minutes of cooking to eliminate the taste of raw flour, but it will take an additional few minutes to brown the flour. Remove from heat and slowly add the desired amount of the liquid in which the meat was cooked, stirring constantly. The amount of liquid added to the *roux* will depend on whether you want a thick or a thin gravy. If you have used two tablespoons of fat drippings and two tablespoons of flour, you will probably want to add at least one and one-half cups of liquid. If additional liquid is needed, you can use stock, wine, consommé, or water. If the telephone rings while you're adding liquid to the *roux*, ignore it, or take the saucepan to the phone with you and *keep stirring*. Return to low heat and stir, to set gravy. Simmer gently for a few minutes, until the gravy has thickened, and then adjust the seasoning.

It is also possible to thicken the liquid in which the meat was cooked by adding a *beurre manié*, a floured butter ball. To make a *beurre manié* place one or two tablespoons of softened butter (more if necessary) on a piece of waxed paper and add an equal amount of flour. Mix the flour into the butter with a rubber spatula or your fingers until you have made a smooth floured butter ball. The ingredients must be thoroughly combined. (You can make several at one time and keep the extra ones in the freezer until needed.) Drop the butter ball (fresh or frozen) into the liquid in which the meat was cooked and stir over moderate heat until the sauce has thickened. Cook gently for a few minutes to eliminate the taste of uncooked flour and then adjust the seasoning.

If you prefer to thicken gravy without adding fat, make a smooth paste of cornstarch and an equal amount of cool cooking liquid, bouillon, or dry wine. Off heat, add slowly to the liquid in which the meat was cooked and stir constantly. Cook gently until the gravy has thickened. You'll need approximately two tablespoons of dissolved cornstarch for each cup of gravy you want to thicken.

Cooking Frozen Meat

Frozen meat may be cooked while it is still frozen, or it may be defrosted prior to cooking. Commercially frozen food, such as "TV Dinners," should be cooked according to package directions.

If meat is to be defrosted before cooking, the best and safest method is to defrost it in the refrigerator in its wrapping, or unwrapped in a microwave oven. Meat should not be defrosted in water unless it is going to be cooked in liquid. After meat has been defrosted, it should be cooked the same way you would cook meat that has not been frozen.

Additional cooking time is required to cook frozen meat. A frozen roast will need approximately one-third to one-half more cooking time than the same roast would require if it had been defrosted before cooking. The additional time needed to cook frozen steaks and chops varies according to the size of the surface area, the thickness of the meat, and the intensity of the heat. Steaks and chops that are defrosted only to the point where they lose their rigidity will be juicier than fully defrosted steaks and chops.

Thick frozen steaks, chops, and ground meat patties must be broiled a greater distance from the heat than those that have been defrosted in order to avoid having the meat become too brown on the outside while it is still cold inside. Meat that is coated with breading should be partially defrosted so the coating will adhere properly to the meat.

When frozen meat is pan-broiled, a preheated skillet should be used so the meat has an opportunity to brown before the surface defrosts and browning is retarded. Once the surface has been browned, the heat should be reduced, and the meat should be turned occasionally during cooking so it will cook evenly.

TIMETABLE FOR DEFROSTING FROZEN MEAT

Meat	In Refrigerator (36° to 40° F.)
Large roast	4 to 7 hrs. per lb.
Small roast	3 to 5 hrs. per lb.
1-inch steak	12 to 14 hours

Cooking Variety Meats

Variety meats, which include brains, heart, kidney, liver, sweetbreads, tongue, and tripe, are usually a good buy for several reasons. Since they are often less in demand than other cuts of meat, they usually are a very economical buy. In addition, variety meats provide excellent sources of many essential nutrients and offer new and interesting variations for the unending task of meal planning. Many cookbooks include an impressive number of tempting recipes for variety meats, along with detailed cooking instructions. Variety meats are more perishable than other meat and should be cooked and served as soon after purchase as possible.

Liver Probably the most popular and well-known variety meat is liver. All varieties of liver are high in nutritive value, and all are delicious when properly cooked. Beef and pork liver are frequently braised or sautéed. Sometimes they are ground for loaves or patties. Calf, veal, and lamb liver are more tender and therefore usually are broiled, pan-broiled, or sautéed.

Kidneys Collections of special recipes often include kidneys because they are considered such a great delicacy by so many people. Veal and lamb kidneys are sometimes left attached to chops and sold as "veal kidney chops" or "lamb English chops." Beef kidneys are less tender than other kidneys and should be cooked in liquid or braised. Lamb and veal kidneys may be broiled or may be wrapped in bacon and cooked on a skewer.

Heart Although it is very flavorful and nutritious, heart is not tender and should be braised or cooked in liquid for three or four hours. Most heart that is available comes from beef or veal. It can be stuffed or diced and added to a stew. It can also be ground and combined with other ground meat for added flavor.

Tongue Another very popular variety meat is tongue, which may be purchased fresh, pickled (corned), smoked, or canned. Tongue is one of the less-tender variety meats and needs long, slow cooking in liquid. Smoked or pickled tongue occasionally requires soaking before cooking. After a tongue has been cooked, the skin is removed, and the tongue may be sliced and served hot or cold with a sweet and sour sauce, a hot mustard sauce, or other spicy sauce. Tongue is also an excellent addition to casseroles and salads.

Tripe Available fresh, pickled, and canned, tripe has a unique delicate flavor. Although it can be purchased fully cooked, tripe is usually only partially cooked and needs additional precooking in salted water. Then it may be served with a well-seasoned tomato sauce, brushed with melted butter and broiled, spread with dressing and baked, dipped in batter and sautéed, creamed, or added to a thick soup like Pepper Pot.

TIMETABLE FOR COOKING VARIETY MEATS

	Broiled	Braised	Cooked in Liquid
LIVER			
Beef			
3 to 4 pounds		2 to 2½ hr.	
Sliced		20 to 25 min.	
Veal (Calf), Sliced	8 to 10 min.		
Pork			
3 to 3½ pounds		1½ to 2 hr.	
Sliced		20 to 25 min.	
Lamb, Sliced	8 to 10 min.		
KIDNEY			
Beef		1½ to 2 hr.	1 to 1½ hr.
Veal	10 to 12 min.	1 to 1½ hr.	¾ to 1 hr.
Pork	10 to 12 min.	1 to 1½ hr.	¾ to 1 hr.
Lamb	10 to 12 min.	¾ to 1 hr.	¾ to 1 hr.
HEART			
Beef			
Whole		3 to 4 hr.	3 to 4 hr.
Sliced		1½ to 2 hr.	
Veal		2½ to 3 hr.	2½ to 3 hr.
Pork		2½ to 3 hr.	2½ to 3 hr.
Lamb		2½ to 3 hr.	2½ to 3 hr.
TONGUE			
Beef			3 to 4 hr.
Veal			2 to 3 hr.
Pork	usually sold ready-to-serve		
Lamb			
TRIPE			
Beef	10 to 15 min.		1 to 1½ hr.
SWEETBREADS	10 to 15 min.	20 to 25 min.	15 to 20 min.
BRAINS	10 to 15 min.	20 to 25 min.	15 to 20 min.

Sweetbreads* The two lobes of the thymus gland are a tender and subtly flavored delicacy called sweetbreads. Since the thymus gland disappears as an animal matures, most sweetbreads come from veal, calf, or young beef. Sweetbreads should be soaked and peeled before cooking and then broiled, sautéed, braised, or cooked in liquid. Since they are very perishable, they should be frozen or precooked, unless they are going to be used immediately. To precook, simmer for thirty minutes in acidulated water (one tablespoon of lemon juice or vinegar for each quart of water). If sweetbreads are cooked in water, the membrane may be removed after cooking. Precooked sweetbreads may be broken into small pieces and scrambled with eggs, reheated in a well-seasoned sauce, breaded and deep-fried, used in a salad, or dipped in butter and broiled.

Brains* Another tender delicacy is brains. Like sweetbreads, they should be frozen or precooked if they are not used immediately after they are purchased. They should be soaked and peeled before cooking and then broiled, sautéed, braised or cooked in liquid. If brains are cooked in water, the membrane may be removed after cooking. Precooked brains may be used in the same way sweetbreads are used.

Cooking Sausage

Cooked smoked sausage links don't require additional cooking but they may be heated in the following ways if desired:

To simmer: Drop sausage links in boiling water, cover, reduce heat and simmer (don't boil) five to ten minutes, depending on the size of the sausage.

To panbroil: Melt a small amount of butter in a heavy skillet and brown the sausage links over moderate heat, turning often. Don't use a fork to turn sausage links; use tongs instead, to avoid piercing them.

*Note: Both sweetbreads and brains require soaking to whiten them. Place them in a bowl of cold water and soak for one and a half to two hours, changing the water several times. Remove from water and gently pull off the membrane. Soak again in cold water to which one tablespoon of vinegar per quart of water has been added. Soak an additional one and a half to two hours, changing water frequently. Drain and remove any remaining membrane.

To broil: Brush each sausage link with butter and broil about three inches from the heat, turning with tongs to insure even browning.

Fresh or uncooked smoked sausage must be cooked.

To panfry: Place sausage links or patties in a cold skillet. Add two to four tablespoons of water, cover tightly, cook slowly over moderate heat five to eight minutes depending on the size or thickness of the sausage. Remove cover and brown slowly, turning often with tongs.

To bake: Arrange sausage links in a single layer in a shallow baking dish. Bake, uncovered, in a 400° F oven twenty to thirty minutes, or until well-done. Turn with tongs to brown evenly. Pour off drippings as they accumulate.

Don't Throw Those Bones Away

No discussion of proper cooking methods is complete without mention of the most neglected item in a meat case or the kitchen: bones.

Bones that are left over after meat has been cooked have an important value many cooks ignore. A ham bone is an essential ingredient of pea soup. Beef ribs that have been saved from a cooked rib roast can be deviled and served with a sauce for a truly delicious meal. Almost all cooked bones, along with scraps of leftover meat, make a delicious and nutritious addition to a hearty soup or to the stock pot.

Aside from nutrition and improved flavor, the use of cooked bones and scraps of leftover meat can provide a big lift for overburdened food budgets. The process of making homemade soup is not complicated. Admittedly, it takes more time than opening a can, but it may cost less in the long run when the principal ingredients are the leftovers from another meal.

Uncooked bones, available inexpensively in most supermarkets, are the essential ingredient of stock. Stock can almost always be substituted for water in a meat, soup, vegetable, sauce, or gravy recipe. In addition to the added flavor stock provides, the nutritive value of food cooked with stock is increased.

There are plenty of fine recipes available for stock. None of them requires a high degree of skill; all of them require time and a very large kettle. No matter what type of stock you make—light, dark, or all-purpose—and regardless of whether you add meat, chicken, vegetables, or seasonings, you must use bones. Cracked beef and veal bones, along with marrow and meat from the shin bone, the shank, and the plate, form the basis of a stock that can be used with almost any meat dish. Lamb and pork bones have a strong and distinct flavor and should be reserved to make stock that will be used with a lamb or pork recipe.

Check your favorite cookbook for a good stock recipe, or use the instructions that follow. Make a big batch, and store it in your refrigerator or freezer. Once you use stock, you will never want to be without it. To make about two quarts of stock, take a few pounds of newly purchased or leftover bones and meat scraps (raw or cooked), spread them out in a large roasting pan and add a few chopped carrots and onions. Place in a 400° F oven for twenty to thirty minutes to brown, turning all ingredients occasionally. Discard fat and scrape browned ingredients into a large kettle. Pour boiling water into roasting pan to scrape up juices. Add to kettle. Add another onion and carrot and a few stalks of celery. Pour in enough cold water to cover everything by two inches. Bring to a simmer and skim off accumulated scum. Add a small amount of salt and a *bouquet garni* (see page 197). Cover partially and simmer at least two or three hours. Strain into a clean container and cool, uncovered. Refrigerate and remove congealed fat.

Don't Forget Leftovers

Someone once said an entire army could subsist for months on what Americans put in their garbage. This may be something of an exaggeration, but it certainly is true that perfectly good food often is thrown away because a busy cook simply doesn't take time to think about ways to use it. Really smart shoppers purposely buy extra meat and include at least one meal using leftovers each week when they plan menus. With a little imagination, even small scraps of meat can be put to excellent use. There are two good reasons for planning menus that make use of leftovers: time and money. Preparing a meal that includes meat you have already cooked can be a tremendous time-saver and utilizing leftovers is a superb budget stretcher.

If you don't want to use leftovers immediately, they can be stored in the refrigerator or freezer, provided they are properly wrapped. Unwrapped meat will dry out. Large pieces of leftover roast can be stored safely in the refrigerator for as long as five days and can be kept frozen for up to three months. Cooked leftover meat that is then ground or cut into small pieces should be stored no longer than three days in the refrigerator or two months in the freezer. Meat that was frozen raw, thawed, and then cooked may be refrozen safely.

Cold, sliced, cooked meat makes excellent sandwiches and the same meat, cut into strips or cubes, can become the basis for a superb salad. Cooked roasts will dry out if reheated in the oven—unless you own a microwave oven with the marvelous capacity for reheating food quickly without drying it out. Slices from a leftover roast can be reheated in gravy or a simple sauce. With a little additional effort, and a good sauce recipe, you can turn leftover meat into an elegant meal. A sharp knife or a good meat grinder can transform leftover meat into cubes or ground meat that can be combined with pasta or potatoes, vegetables, and a sauce to make a delicious and nourishing casserole. Small scraps of leftover meat are a marvelous and flavorful addition to soup, whether homemade or from a can or package. Leftover bones are an essential basis for many homemade soups. Anyone who has learned the delights of cooking with homemade stock has also learned that leftover bones and scraps of meat add immeasurably to the stockpot.

Planning ahead, and buying enough extra meat to provide leftovers, is unquestionably an effective way to stretch meat dollars. If you buy the right grade and the right cut for a given recipe, especially when meat is on sale, you will discover very quickly that meat does not have to take up a disproportionate amount of your food budget.

The Final Touch

The way food looks when it is served is almost as important as the way it tastes. Select a dish or platter that is a suitable size for the food you are serving. A small roast, sitting on a large carving board, will look lost. People are likely to react by asking for unusually small helpings because they may be concerned about whether there is enough meat to go around. On the other hand, a large roast served on a small carving board or platter, surrounded by other food, may look all right; but it means certain disaster for a clean tablecloth. The carver must have enough room available on the platter to carve the meat properly.

If your entree includes a sauce or gravy, don't drown the meat in liquid. Put the extra gravy in a separate smaller dish that can be passed around.

Inexpensive oven-to-table casserole dishes are available in attractive patterns and can be a great help in reducing kitchen clean-up. But if food has spilled on the outside of the dish during cooking, be sure to take time to wipe off the casserole before you bring it to the table.

Plan menus with eye-appeal in mind. If you serve a pale meat, such as veal, and want to have a white vegetable like cauliflower at the same meal, serve green spinach noodles instead of white noodles for added color on the dinner plate. Interestingly enough, most meals that have good color balance also have good nutritional balance.

The simplest dish can look elegant if you take a few extra minutes to add a garnish before you bring it to the table. A garnish does not have to be a delicately sculptured food carving. It can be just a few sprigs of crisp fresh parsley, neatly cut lemon wedges, or even a dash of paprika.

Esthetically served food is always appreciated. In addition to making dinner a pleasant visual experience, attractively served food can be helpful in persuading an invalid to eat "just a bit more," and can go a long way toward tempting a hesitant youngster to "try just a taste." The effort involved is often minimal; the rewards can be substantial.

6

Cooking in the Great Outdoors

The earliest barbecues in America took place long before Columbus reached these shores, and settlers in the New World learned Indian methods of barbecuing native food soon after they arrived. Then, as now, the desire to cook outside had its origin in an effort to escape the heat of an open hearth in a hut or colonial kitchen during hot weather. But even the advent of modern air conditioning has not dimmed the appeal of a picnic or barbecue. Some people are lucky enough to live in a climate that permits them to cook out-of-doors most of the year. But for a great many people, the chance to eat out-of-doors means a welcome change in the season or a special trip to the country. One of the nicest things about outdoor eating is the opportunity it provides for easy, informal entertaining. There are similarities in the way meat is handled for indoor and outdoor cooking, but there are some differences, too. If meat is to be cooked properly, these differences should be taken into consideration.

Choosing the Meat

Almost any cut of meat suitable for roasting, broiling, pan-broiling, or pan-frying may be cooked out-of-doors over hot coals. Roasts should be as regular in shape as possible to insure even cooking. Steaks and chops should be at least three-quarters of an inch thick. Cubes of meat to be cooked on a skewer must be cut into uniform-size pieces.

There is something about the wonderful aroma of a barbecue wafting by that increases most appetites enormously. So it is important to adjust your estimate of the amount of meat you will need accordingly. If you are serving a boneless cut, you probably will need between one-third and one-half pound per person, depending on the type of meat and on how much other food you plan to serve. You will need between three-quarters of a pound and one pound per person if you are serving a bone-in cut.

When planning a menu, you must consider the amount of time available to prepare the fire and cook the meat. Most meat takes longer to cook over coals than it takes to cook indoors. Outdoors, a large boneless roast may take from three and one-half to five hours, depending on its size, the heat maintained, and the internal temperature desired. Spareribs can take from one hour to one and one-half hours. The time needed to grill meat varies from six to eight minutes for a frankfurter to fifteen or twenty minutes per side for a two-inch steak cooked medium rare.

How to Cook Outdoors

Outdoor cooking equipment is as varied as indoor cooking equipment. Meat can be cooked on anything from a small pit dug in the ground to an elaborate motorized barbecue grill. Unless cooking facilities are homemade, you probably have the manufacturer's instructions on the proper use of your equipment. These instructions should be kept in a safe place and followed carefully. If you lose them, or find them inadequate, follow the methods suggested below for safe and satisfactory barbecuing.

- Line the bottom of the grill with heavy duty aluminum foil. It will make clean-up easier and help keep the grill in top condition.

- Make a fire base of gravel (or a commercial equivalent) one to three inches deep, to permit the fire to "breathe," and to provide maximum heat from the coals. If the base of the grill has a rounded bottom, use enough fire base to make a level bed to the edge of the bowl. After four or five barbecues, the fire base should be washed to remove drippings and accumulated ash. Don't use your grill again until the fire base is thoroughly dry because gravel may explode if it is heated while still wet.

- Be sure to light the fire well in advance of the time you plan to start cooking. You'll need a good bed of glowing hot—not flaming—coals when you begin to cook.

- If you use an electric fire starter, arrange the charcoal briquets in a flat pile. Put the heating element on the charcoal, then add more briquets. In about ten minutes, you will see a gray ash on the briquets near the heating element. Disconnect the starter (be careful, it will be very hot!) and put it aside. It will take approximately fifteen minutes for the briquets to be well-covered with gray ash. Spread the coals about one-half inch apart, tap them gently to remove some of the ash, and start cooking.

- If you prefer, use commercially-prepared flammable liquids or jellies as starters. Do *not* use gasoline. Build a pyramid of charcoal briquets in the firebowl. Pour or squirt a few ounces of the liquid over the charcoal or force a few teaspoonful of jelly into the crevices between the briquets. Be absolutely certain you put the cap back on the container and place it a safe distance from the grill before you light the fire. The fire will be ready to use in about thirty minutes, when the briquets are covered with gray ash. Spread the briquets, tap them, as above, and start cooking.

- *Never, under any circumstances, add lighter fluid or jelly to a flaming fire, or even to hot coals.* Flames can easily feed back to the can, causing a serious accident. Don't take a chance!

- You can also use packaged, treated charcoal briquets as a starter. Place the package underneath a pile of loose briquets and light the package with a long match. This method takes about forty-five minutes to get the fire ready for cooking. Be sure the treated coals are completely burned before you start cooking in order to avoid an unpleasant taste in the food.

  If you want to add the flavor of smoke to the meat, the best method is to use wood chips. Soak hickory, oak, apple, or cherry chips in water for at least one hour before using them. Soaking will provide a maximum amount of smoke and, at the same time, will prevent the chips from burning. Add a few soaked chips at a time to the charcoal during cooking. If the chips burn, replace them with wet chips. The flavor of smoke can also be added to meat through the use of liquid smoke in marinades and basting sauces. Special smoker-type barbecue units are available with hoods which can be closed during cooking to retain both heat and smoke.

Cooking Hints

Low to moderate temperatures are best for cooking meat either out-of-doors or in the kitchen. Coals should glow rather than flame. The amount of heat and the rate of cooking can be controlled by adjusting the distance of the grill or rotisserie from the coals. Remember, heat can be intensified by the wind.

An essential part of many barbecue recipes is a sauce which is often used to baste meat during cooking. Basting may be done throughout the entire cooking period. However, if sugar or any other ingredient that burns easily is used in the sauce, it's better to baste during the final half hour of cooking only.

A meat thermometer should be used to help determine when the meat is done. If meat is being cooked on a rotisserie, the thermometer must clear the cooking unit and drip pan as the meat turns.

Whether meat is cooked indoors or out-of-doors, it will be easier to carve if it is allowed to "set" after roasting. Remove it from the heat when the thermometer registers five to ten degrees below the internal temperature desired. If you're cooking on a spit, be sure to remove the hot rotisserie rod, too.

Special Tips for Rotisserie Cooking

Start the fire with a small amount of charcoal and add more during cooking as needed. Arrange the lit briquets at the rear of the fire bowl and knock off the gray ash. Control the heat during cooking by adjusting the height of the fire box, or by adding or removing briquets. Place a drip pan, which can be made from heavy duty aluminum foil, under the meat and adjust the position of the drip pan to catch the juices as the meat turns.

Insert the rotisserie rod lengthwise through the center of a roast and test for good balance by rotating the rod in the palm of your hands. Fasten the meat securely, so it turns only when the rod turns and does not wobble.

The rotisserie rod should be woven in and out of ribs to form accordian folds. Keep the ribs in balance for smooth turning and even cooking.

Kabobs should be cut into uniform-size pieces and placed on a rotisserie rod with other food cut to the same size. If desired, the kabobs may be marinated before cooking. Food that will take longer to cook than the meat should be parboiled or partially precooked before it is added to the rod with the meat. This is always a good rule to follow when combinations of food are cooked on a skewer because it eliminates the problem of either overcooked meat or undercooked vegetables.

7

Health and Nutrition

It's not surprising that meat continues to be a favorite food among most Americans and throughout a large part of the world because the more we learn about the advantages of eating meat, the more appealing it becomes.

Surprising as it may be to many people, meat is not high in cholesterol. The body manufactures more cholesterol than that which is contributed to the body through food. While the medical controversy over the effects of cholesterol rages back and forth, meat continues to be mistakenly identified as high in cholesterol. However, there is no disagreement about the fact that meat is low in calories and high in nutritive value.

Meat is included in the diets of six-week old infants and is still an important part of the diet when the infant becomes a senior citizen. It is included in so many diets because it is almost completely digestible. Even the old wives tale that "pork is hard to digest" has been disproved by many food studies. Proteins from meat are at least 97 percent digested, and fat from meat is at least 96 percent digested.

An important factor in controlling excessive eating is choosing foods that are filling and satisfying. The more quickly a food is digested, the more quickly a person feels hungry after eating. Fats, even the small amounts found in marbled meat, tend to slow down the passage of food through the stomach, which in turn slows down the rate of digestion. As a result, the feeling of hunger usually does not return quickly when meat is included in a meal.

Psychologically, meat is often an aid to the digestion of other food. The wonderful aroma of properly cooked meat can help to initiate the flow of important digestive juices in the body. The flow of these juices is a significant factor in the digestion of all food eaten.

CHOLESTEROL CONTENT OF FOOD

	Raw	Mg.*
Egg, (Whole)		550
Pork		70
Beef		70
Chicken (Skinless)		60
Fish		70
Lamb		70
Veal		90

*Cholesterol per 100 g. (Approx. 3½ oz.) Edible Portion.

139

Daily Food Guide

**MEAT GROUP
Two or more
servings**

THE GROUP INCLUDES:

beef	sausages
pork	ready-to-serve meat
veal	poultry
lamb	eggs
variety meats	fish

. . . AND THESE ALTERNATES:

dry peas	nuts
dry beans	peanut butter

COUNT AS A SERVING: 2 to 3 ounces of lean cooked meat, poultry or fish (without bone or fat), 2 eggs, 1 cup cooked dry beans or peas, or 4 tablespoons peanut butter.

MILK GROUP

THE GROUP INCLUDES:

whole milk	whole or nonfat dry milk
skim milk	evaporated milk
buttermilk	yogurt

Children under 8	2 or more cups
Children 8 to 12	3 or more cups
Teenagers	4 or more cups
Adults	2 or more cups

. . . AND THESE ALTERNATES AS CALCIUM EQUIVALENTS:

cheese   ice cream
1 slice or 1-inch cube of Cheddar-type cheese = ¾ cup milk
½ cup cottage cheese = ⅓ cup milk
2 tablespoons cream cheese = 1 tablespoon milk
¼ pt. or ½ cup ice cream = ¼ cup milk

**BREAD-CEREALS
GROUP
Four or more
servings**

THE GROUP INCLUDES: enriched, whole grain or restored products:

bread	rice
rolls	macaroni, spaghetti, noodles
quick breads	cornmeal
cereals, ready-to-eat	grits
and cooked	

COUNT AS A SERVING: 1 slice bread, 1 ounce ready-to-eat cereal, ½ to ¾ cup cooked cereal, cornmeal, grits, macaroni, spaghetti, noodles and rice.

THE SERVINGS SHOULD INCLUDE:

—A citrus fruit, other fruit, or vegetable that provides vitamin C:

orange	**fresh pineapple**
grapefruit	**honeydew melon**
cantaloupe	**tomato**
strawberries	**cabbage**
mango	**Brussels sprouts**
papaya	**broccoli**
guava	**green pepper**
watermelon	**potato, cooked in skin**
tangerine	

—A dark-green vegetable, deep-yellow vegetable, or fruit that provides vitamin A (at least every other day):

carrot	**collards**
sweet potato	**kale**
apricots	**spinach**
cantaloupe	**broccoli**
pumpkin	**turnip greens**
persimmon	**garden cress**
winter squash	**mustard greens**
mango	**dandelion greens**
chard, leaves	**beet greens**

—Other vegetables and fruit:

apple	**corn**
banana	**cucumber**
berries	**green beans**
cherries	**lettuce**
grapes	**lima beans**
peach	**onion**
pear	**peas**
plum	**potato**
asparagus	**rhubarb**
beets	**rutabaga**
cauliflower	**turnips**
celery	

VEGETABLE-FRUIT GROUP
Four or more servings

COUNT AS A SERVING: ½ cup vegetable or fruit or a portion as ordinarily served such as a medium apple, orange, banana or potato or a half grapefruit or cantaloup.

Plus . . . Fats, Sweets and Other Foods
Butter and magarine, salad dressing, jams, jellies, and other sweets or fats may be added to meals to help make them more satisfying. Individual energy needs and the quantity of food eaten from the four groups determine the amount of "extras" that may be included in the diet without adding undue weight.

In recent years scientists and nutritionists have learned a great deal about the nutritional value of various foods as well as the nutritional requirements of the human body. To simplify this information and make it easily understandable to everyone, foods were arranged in groups, each group providing its own special contribution to human dietary needs. When meals include the recommended amount from *each* group, a diet is properly balanced. In the familiar Daily Food Guide, food is divided into four categories—one of which is meat. No single food or group of foods can meet all nutritional needs alone. Foods from each group are necessary, and they work together to build and maintain healthy bodies.

The Nutrients Provided By Meat

Different foods provide different nutrients. The body requires all nutrients to remain healthy and to grow. Meat is unique because it provides so many necessary nutrients in substantial quantities.

Proteins All life requires protein. It is the chief tissue builder, the basic substance of every cell in the body. Protein is made up of smaller units called amino acids. When food is eaten, proteins are broken down (digested) into amino acids, which are then rearranged to form the many special and distinct proteins in the body. Proteins in food are usually made up of eighteen or more amino acids. The body can make its own supply of more than half of them but the others must come from food.

Although proteins from soybeans, legumes, chickpeas, and peanuts are almost as good as proteins derived from animal sources, proteins from cereal grains, vegetables, and fruit do not provide as good an assortment of amino acids as animal proteins. Therefore, in order to be certain you are getting an adequate amount of protein in your diet, it's a good idea to have some food from an animal source at every meal.

PROTEIN CONTENT OF COOKED MEAT*

(100 grams, lean plus marble with separable fat removed except where indicated)

	Protein (grams)		Protein (grams)
BEEF		**PORK**	
Steak		Chop, loin, center cut[2]	34.6
Club	25.7		
Flank	33.4	**Steak**	
Porterhouse	25.4	Blade	29.0
Rib	25.5	Fresh ham	37.0
Round, bottom	35.5		
Round, top	38.8	**Roast**	
Sirloin	25.5	Boston butt	25.4
T-bone	25.3	Picnic shoulder, fresh	25.9
Tenderloin	26.0	Ham, cured butt end	
		(smoked)	25.1
Roast		Ham, cured shank end	
Sirloin tip	29.4	(smoked)	25.6
Standing rib	22.3	Sirloin	30.0
		Tenderloin[1]	30.6
Pot-roast		Shoulder butt, cured	
Arm	33.0	(smoked)	22.6
Blade	34.6		
Heel of round	31.2	**Other cuts**[1]	
Rolled neck	30.5	Bacon, Canadian-style	30.3
Standing rump	32.0	Bacon, regular sliced	32.9
		Bacon, thick sliced	34.5
Other cuts		Sausage, link	20.4
Brisket, thick end	24.6		
Brisket, thin end	26.3	**LAMB**	
Ground beef[1]	25.6	**Chop**	
Ground beef, extra lean[1]	30.1	Arm	25.7
Short ribs[1]	24.4	Blade	27.4
Stew meat, chuck[1]	22.5	Loin	27.1
Stew meat, round[1]	32.5	Rib	25.5
		Roast, leg	28.2
		Riblets	23.5
VEAL			
Chop[2]			
Loin	34.2		
Rib	33.6		
Steak[2]			
Arm	35.6		
Blade	33.3		
Cutlet, round	38.1		
Sirloin	34.8		
Roast			
Rump	30.6		
Sirloin	27.9		
Stew meat, breast[1]	27.9		

*Ruth M. Leverton and George V. Odell, *The Nutritive Value of Cooked Meat* (Miscellaneous Publication MP-49; Stillwater: Oklahoma Agricultural Experiment Station, Oklahoma State University, 1959).

[1]Entire portion, separable fat not removed

[2]All lean

PROXIMATE PROTEIN COMPOSITION OF
100 GRAMS OF COOKED VARIETY MEATS*

	Protein (grams)		Protein (grams)
BEEF		**PORK**	
Brain	11.5	Brain	12.2
Heart	28.9	Heart	23.6
Kidney	24.7	Kidney	25.4
Liver	22.9	Liver	21.6
Lung	20.3	Lung	16.6
Pancreas	27.1	Pancreas (Sweetbreads)	28.5
Spleen	25.1	Spleen	28.2
Thymus	20.5	Tongue	24.1
Tongue	22.2		
VEAL		**LAMB**	
Brain	10.5	Brain	12.7
Heart	26.3	Heart	21.7
Kidney	26.3	Kidney	23.1
Liver	21.5	Liver	23.7
Lung	18.8	Lung	20.9
Pancreas	29.1	Pancreas	23.3
Spleen	23.9	Spleen	27.3
Thymus (Sweetbreads)	18.4	Tongue	21.5
Tongue	26.2		

*Lilia Kizlaitis, Carol Diebel and A. 5. Siedler, "Nutrient Content of Variety Meats II. The Effects of Cooking on the Vitamin A, Ascorbic Acid, Iron and Proximate Composition," *Food Technology* (Volume 18:103, 1964).

PROXIMATE PROTEIN COMPOSITION OF 100
GRAMS OF CURED AND PROCESSED MEATS*†

	Protein (grams)		Protein (grams)
Bacon	9.1	Salami	23.9
Bologna	14.8	Salami, cooked	17.1
Braunschweiger	15.2	Salt pork	3.9
Corned beef	15.8	Country-style sausage	16.2
Dried beef	34.3	Polish sausage	16.4
Dutch loaf	15.0	Pork sausage, fresh	10.8
Frankfurter	15.2	Smoked sausage link	15.4
Head cheese	15.1	Summer sausage	23.5
Kolbase	13.5	Thuringer	17.7
Liver sausage	16.7		

*Charlotte Chatfield and G. Adams, *Proximate Composition of American Food Materials* (U. S. Department of Agriculture Circ. No. 549; Washington, D. C.: U. S. Government Printing Office, 1940).

B. S. Schweigert and Barbara J. Payne, *A Summary of the Nutrient Content of Meat* (Bulletin No. 30; Chicago: American Meat Institute Foundation, 1956).

†Analyses were on samples as purchased, without further cooking.

Vitamins play an indispensable role in the release of energy from food for use by the body. This is one of the major reasons increased vitamin intake is often recommended for people who are lacking in energy. Vitamins also promote normal growth of different kinds of body tissue, and they are essential to the proper functioning of nerves, muscles, digestion, and healthy skin.

Vitamins

There are eleven B vitamins. Six of them—thiamin, riboflavin, niacin, folacin, vitamin B_6, and vitamin B_{12}—are considered essential to a healthy, balanced diet. Meat is an excellent source of B vitamins. It ranks as the principal dietary source of most of them and is a major source of vitamin B_{12}.

Vitamin C, which is also called ascorbic acid, helps to form and maintain cementing material that holds body cells together and strengthens the walls of blood vessels. It also assists in normal tooth and bone formation and aids in the healing of wounds. Liver is a superb source of vitamin C. Small amounts of this vitamin are also found in kidneys.

B VITAMIN CONTENT OF 100 GRAMS OF CURED AND PROCESSED MEATS*†

	Thiamin (mg)	Riboflavin (mg)	Niacin (mg)
Bacon	.19	.10	0.8
Bologna	.31	.30	3.1
Braunschweiger	.13	1.40	8.1
Canadian-style bacon	.57	.18	2.8
Corned beef	.05	.10	1.7
Dried beef	.07	.32	3.8
Dutch loaf	.31	.17	3.2
Frankfurter	.23	.24	2.7
Head cheese	.08	.12	1.1
Kolbase	.34	.19	3.1
Liver sausage	.20	1.30	5.7
Pork sausage link	.40	.15	2.3
Salami	.25	.21	2.9
Salami, cooked	.26	.21	4.5
Salt pork	.18	.04	0.9
Sandwich meat	.43	.18	3.6
Sausage link‡	.22	.19	3.1
Summer sausage	.46	.36	4.1
Thuringer	.12	.23	4.2

*Schweigert and Payne, *A Summary of the Nutrient Content of Meat.*
†Analyses were on samples as purchased, without further cooking.
‡Beef and pork.

B VITAMIN CONTENT OF COOKED MEAT*

(100 grams, lean plus marble with separable fat removed except where indicated)

Cut Portion	Thiamin (mg)	Riboflavin (mg)	Niacin (mg)	Pantothenic Acid (mg)	Vitamin B_6 (mg)	Vitamin B_{12} (mcg)
BEEF						
Steak						
Round, bottom[2]	0.13	0.33	5.7	0.63	0.45	1.7
Round, top	0.10	0.31	5.7	0.47	0.50	2.1
Sirloin	0.10	0.46	3.3	—	0.41	3.0
T-bone	0.10	0.12	6.1	0.86	—	1.4
Roast, standing rib	0.06	0.21	4.0	0.54	0.34	2.3
Pot-roast, standing rump	0.10	0.23	4.3	0.60	0.38	2.2
Other cuts						
Brisket, thick end	0.05	0.23	3.9	0.52	0.27	1.5
Ground beef[1]	0.16	0.18	5.6	0.44	0.46	1.3
Ground beef, extra lean[1]	0.22	0.13	8.2	0.45	0.65	0.9
Stew meat, round[1]	0.10	0.25	5.1	0.49	0.22	3.0
VEAL						
Chop, loin[2]	0.21	0.32	7.1	0.50	0.43	2.7
Steak, cutlet, round[2]	0.14	0.37	7.3	0.50	0.50	2.2
Roast						
Rump	0.16	0.20	8.2	0.71	0.48	2.5
Sirloin[2]	0.18	0.26	8.7	0.84	0.52	2.7
PORK						
Chop, loin center cut[2]	1.18	0.19	5.5	0.40	0.48	1.1
Steak, fresh ham[2]	0.68	0.32	5.3	0.49	0.44	1.4
Roast						
Ham, cured (smoked)						
shank end	0.78	0.24	4.1	0.57	0.34	1.2
Sirloin[2]	1.27	0.34	4.6	0.88	0.56	1.2
Other cuts						
Bacon, Canadian-style	0.99	0.15	4.6	0.44	0.55	1.2
Sausage, link	0.76	0.20	4.0	0.56	0.19	1.4
LAMB						
Chop, loin[2]	0.21	0.33	7.9	0.59	0.33	2.4
Roast, leg[2]	0.23	0.31	7.3	0.61	0.32	3.1

*Leverton and Odell, *The Nutritive Value of Cooked Meat.*
[1]Entire portion, separable fat not removed   [2]All lean

VITAMIN CONTENT OF 100 GRAMS OF FRESH VARIETY MEATS*

	Thia-min (mg)	Ribo-flavin (mg)	Niacin (mg)	Vita-min B₆ (mg)	Panto-thenic Acid (mg)	Biotin (mcg)	Fola-cin (mcg)	Vita-min B₁₂ (mcg)	Vita-min A Value† (IU)	Ascor-bic Acid‡ (mg)
BEEF										
Brain	0.12	0.22	3.6	0.16	2.5	6.1	12	4.7	Nil	19.2
Heart	0.24	0.84	6.6	0.29	2.3	7.3	110	9.7	Trace	7.0
Kidney	0.28	1.9	5.3	0.39	3.4	92.0	41	28.0	880	10.4
Liver	0.23	3.3	14.0	0.74	7.3	100.0	81	65.0	12,709	22.4
Lung	0.11	0.36	4.0	0.07	1.0	5.9	—	3.3	Nil	38.5
Pancreas	0.14	0.34	3.1	0.20	3.8	14.0	—	4.8	Nil	13.7
Spleen	0.13	0.28	4.2	0.12	1.2	5.7	—	5.1	Nil	45.5
Tongue	0.16	0.28	3.9	0.13	2.0	3.3	—	—	Nil	3.3
Veal liver	0.52	3.3	16.5	0.30	6.0	75.0	46	—	13,530	26.3
PORK										
Brain	0.16	0.28	4.3	—	2.8	—	—	2.8	Nil	13.5
Heart	0.31	0.81	7.3	0.35	2.5	18.0	—	2.4	Trace	5.0
Kidney	0.26	1.9	8.6	0.55	3.1	130.0	—	6.6	230	14.2
Liver	0.25	3.0	14.0	0.51	6.6	85.0	74	23.0	15,142	21.6
Lung	0.09	0.27	3.4	—	0.9	—	—	—	Nil	13.1
Pancreas (Sweetbreads)	0.11	0.46	3.5	—	4.6	—	—	6.5	Nil	15.3
Spleen	0.13	0.30	4.3	—	1.1	—	—	4.1	Nil	30.0
LAMB										
Brain	0.15	0.26	3.7	—	2.6	—	—	7.3	Trace	19.4
Heart	0.31	0.86	4.6	—	3.0	—	—	5.2	Trace	7.3
Kidney	0.38	2.2	6.8	—	4.3	—	—	26.0	279	12.9
Liver	0.29	3.9	12.0	0.37	8.1	130.0	—	35.0	76,756	25.0
Lung	0.11	0.47	4.7	—	1.2	—	—	5.0	89	31.4
Pancreas	0.13	0.50	3.9	—	3.5	—	—	19.0	Nil	17.5
Spleen	0.09	0.27	4.7	—	1.5	—	—	6.7	Nil	23.2

*Schweigert and Payne, *A Summary of the Nutrient Content of Meat.*

C. H. Lushbough, Jean M. Weichman and B. S. Schweigert, "The Retention of Vitamin B₆ in Meat During Cooking," *Journal of Nutrition,* 67 (1959).

A. J. Siedler, Lilia Kizlaitis and Carol Deibel, *Nutritional Quality of Variety Meats—Proximate Composition, Vitamin A, Vitamin C and Iron Content of Raw and Cooked Variety Meats* (Bulletin No. 54; Chicago: American Meat Institute Foundation, 1963).

Kizlaitis and others, "Nutrien Content of Variety Meats," *Food Technology.*

†Insignificant loss in cooking.

‡Relatively large amounts of ascorbic acid are found in all cooked liver, brains and especially in veal thymus (sweetbreads) and pork pancreas (sweetbreads).

Minerals Many minerals are required to give strength and rigidity to certain body tissues and to help with a variety of vital body functions. Iron, a mineral of major importance to good health, teams with certain amino acids in protein to build and maintain hemoglobin, which carries oxygen to body tissues and is responsible for the red color of blood. Iron also helps the cells obtain energy from food. Meat, particularly liver, is the best available source for iron.

MINERAL CONTENT OF COOKED MEAT*
(100 grams, lean plus marble with separable fat removed except where indicated)

Cut Portion	Calcium (mg)	Phosphorus (mg)	Sodium (mg)	Potassium (mg)	Magnesium (mg)
BEEF					
Steak					
Round, bottom	12.7	228	44.4	484	24.8
Round, top	8.4	255	41.8	493	26.2
Sirloin	14.8	226	45.9	436	21.0
T-bone	10.7	181	51.6	398	19.8
Roast, standing rib	7.5	164	53.6	413	18.6
Pot-roast, standing rump	8.3	197	54.1	386	20.4
Other cuts					
Brisket, thick end	11.5	173	54.9	300	15.9
Ground beef[1]	7.3	220	47.4	450	21.3
Ground beef, extra lean[1]	16.1	271	47.5	558	26.2
Stew meat, round[1]	13.4	190	60.3	498	20.8
VEAL					
Chop, loin[2]	8.5	261	66.3	475	21.4
Steak, cutlet[2]	12.1	318	61.6	606	25.2
Roast					
Rump	9.1	247	74.3	509	20.6
Sirloin	9.1[2]	251	64.1[2]	580[2]	21.5
PORK					
Chop, loin[2]	12.1	263	59.6	568	25.3
Steak, fresh ham[2]	7.3	269	71.8	510	28.0
Roast					
Ham, cured (smoked)					
shank end	7.7	186	862.8	398	19.5
Sirloin, fresh	5.4[2]	262	55.0[2]	509[2]	23.8
Other cuts[1]					
Bacon, Canadian-style	18.8	218	2,555	432	25.7
Bacon, regular sliced	15.4	231	1,077	241	24.7
Bacon, thick sliced	9.8	220	852	222	22.7
Sausage, link	18.8	162	958	333	17.0
LAMB					
Chop, loin	8.2[2]	214	82.9[2]	485[2]	24.1
Roast, leg	8.2[2]	215	84.9[2]	512[2]	23.6

*Leverton and Odell, *The Nutritive Value of Cooked Meat.*
[1]Entire portion, separable fat not removed   [2]All lean

MINERAL CONTENT OF 100 GRAMS
OF FRESH VARIETY MEATS*

	Calcium (mg)	Phosphorus (mg)	Iron† (mg)	Sodium (mg)	Potassium (mg)
BEEF					
Brain	10	312	2.4	125	219
Heart	5	195	4.0	86	193
Kidney	11	219	7.4	176	225
Liver	8	352	6.5	136	281
Lung	—	216	8.4	—	—
Pancreas	—	270	2.9	—	—
Spleen	—	272	10.6	—	—
Thymus	14	393	2.1	96	360
Tongue	8	182	2.1	73	197
Tripe	127	86	1.6	72	9
VEAL					
Brain	10	312	2.4	125	219
Heart	3	160	3.0	94	208
Kidney	—	—	4.0	—	—
Liver	8	333	8.8	73	281
Lung	—	—	5.0	—	—
Pancreas	—	326	2.1	—	—
Spleen	—	272	10.6	—	—
Thymus (Sweetbreads)	—	—	2.0	—	—
Tongue	—	—	3.1	—	—
Tripe	—	—	10.0	—	—
PORK					
Brain	10	312	2.4	125	219
Chitterlings	—	—	2.3	—	—
Heart	3	131	3.3	54	106
Kidney	11	218	6.7	115	178
Liver	10	356	19.2	73	261
Lung	—	—	18.9	—	—
Pancreas (Sweetbreads)	11	282	1.0	44	217
Spleen	—	298	29.4	—	—
Tongue	29	186	1.4	—	—
LAMB					
Brain	10	312	2.4	125	219
Heart	11	249	—	—	—
Kidney	13	218	7.6	200	230
Liver	10	349	10.9	52	202
Lung	—	180	6.4	—	—
Pancreas	—	—	2.5	—	—
Spleen	—	—	60.1	—	—
Tongue	—	147	3.1	—	—
Tripe	—	—	2.4	—	—

*Bernice K. Watt and Annabel L. Merrill, *Composition of Foods—Raw, Processed, Prepared* (U. S. Department of Agriculture Handbook No. 8; Washington, D.C.: U. S. Government Printing Office, 1963).
Schweigert and Payne, *A Summary of the Nutrient Content of Meat.*
Siedler and others, *Nutritional Quality of Variety Meats.*
Kizlaitis and others, "Nutrient Content of Variety Meats," *Food Technology.*
†In general 70 per cent or more of the iron is retained in cooking, with liver retaining 90 to 100 per cent.

MINERAL CONTENT OF 100 GRAMS OF
CURED AND PROCESSED MEATS*†

	Calcium (mg)	Phosphorus (mg)	Iron (mg)	Sodium (mg)	Potassium (mg)
Bacon	13	108	0.8	680	130
Bologna	9	160	2.2	1,300	230
Corned beef	9	125	2.4	1,300	60
Dried beef	20	404	5.1	4,300	200
Frankfurter	9	164	2.3	1,100	140
Liver sausage	9	238	5.4	—	—
Pork sausage	6	116	1.6	740	420
Salt pork	2	42	0.6	1,800	27

*Schweigert and Payne, *A Summary of the Nutrient Content of Meat.*
†Analyses were on samples as purchased, without further cooking.

Calories, Carbohydrates, and Fats

A calorie is a unit of measure for the energy required by the body and provided by food. The number of calories individuals need for energy depends on their age, sex, and the amount of exercise they get. The energy must be provided by food. If food supplies more calories than the body uses, the excess is stored as body fat.

Although millions of weight-conscious people have a general idea of the calorie content of food, relatively few people understand the nutritive value of food. One nutrition expert focused attention on this problem by suggesting that we "choose our calories by the company they keep." By "company" the nutritionist meant the nutritional value of food.

Calories come from three sources—carbohydrates, fats, and protein. Current surveys indicate that about half the calories in the average person's diet come from carbohydrates, 13 to 15 percent from protein, and the remainder from fats. All three nutrients are essential to a healthy diet, but many experts feel weight control can be effected by a more moderate intake of fat and a slightly increased intake of carbohydrates and protein to meet energy needs.

Medical and nutrition authorities strongly caution against drastic diet modification except under the supervision of a physician. They recommend a well-rounded diet, similar to the diet outlined in the Daily Food Guide, which contains moderate amounts of both saturated and unsaturated fats. It is important to remember that fat, along with other nutrients, is essential to a healthy diet.

CALORIE AND FAT CONTENT OF COOKED MEAT*
(100 grams, lean plus marble with separable fat removed except where indicated)

Cut Portion	Energy (Calories)			Fat (grams)
	From Protein	From Fat	Total	
BEEF				
Steak				
Club	110	170	280	18.8
Flank	143	92	235	10.2
Porterhouse	108	134	242	14.8
Rib	109	153	262	17.0
Round, bottom	152	86	238	9.5
Round, top	166	63	229	7.0
Sirloin	109	99	208	11.0
T-bone	107	140	247	15.5
Tenderloin	111	113	224	12.5
Roast				
Sirloin tip	126	60	186	6.7
Standing rib	95	190	285	21.0
Pot-roast				
Arm	141	122	263	13.5
Blade	147	151	298	16.7
Heel of round	134	87	221	9.7
Rolled neck	130	116	246	12.8
Standing rump	137	98	235	10.9
Other cuts				
Brisket, thick end	105	199	304	22.1
Brisket, thin end	112	200	312	22.2
Ground beef[1]	109	154	263	17.1
Ground beef, extra lean[1]	128	35	163	3.9
Short ribs	104	299	403	33.2
Stew meat, chuck[1]	96	325	421	36.0
Stew meat, round[1]	138	122	260	13.5
VEAL				
Chop[2]				
Loin	146	61	207	6.7
Rib	144	71	215	7.9
Steak[2]				
Arm	152	48	200	5.4
Blade	142	69	211	7.7
Cutlet, round	163	39	202	4.3
Sirloin	149	55	204	6.1
Roast				
Rump	131	44	175	4.9
Sirloin	119	57	176	6.3
Stew meat, breast[1]	119	227	346	25.2

*Leverton and Odell, *The Nutritive Value of Cooked Meat.*
[1]Entire portion, separable fat not removed
[2]All lean portion

CALORIE AND FAT CONTENT OF COOKED MEAT*
(100 grams, lean plus marble with separable fat removed except where indicated)

Cut Portion	Energy (Calories)			Fat (grams)
	From Protein	From Fat	Total	
PORK				
Chop, loin center cut[2]	148	102	250	11.3
Steak				
Blade	124	153	277	17.0
Fresh ham	158	79	237	8.8
Roast				
Boston butt	109	174	283	19.3
Picnic shoulder, fresh	111	135	246	15.0
Ham, cured (smoked) butt end	108	97	205	10.8
Ham, cured (smoked) shank end	110	124	234	13.8
Sirloin	128	99	227	11.0
Tenderloin[1]	130	109	239	12.1
Shoulder butt, cured (smoked)	97	221	318	24.5
Other cuts[1]				
Bacon, Canadian-style	129	131	260	14.5
Bacon, regular sliced	141	543	684	60.2
Bacon, thick sliced	147	524	671	58.1
Sausage, link	87	334	421	37.0
LAMB				
Chop				
Arm	110	142	252	15.7
Blade	117	163	280	18.1
Loin	116	107	223	11.9
Rib	109	182	291	20.2
Roast, leg	120	75	195	8.3
Riblets	100	299	399	33.2

CALORIE AND FAT CONTENT OF
100 GRAMS OF FRESH AND COOKED VARIETY MEATS*

| | Energy (Calories) | | | | | | Fat (grams) | |
| | Fresh | | | Cooked† | | | | |
	From Protein	From Fat	Total	From Protein	From Fat	Total	Fresh	Cooked†
BEEF								
Brain	44	78	122	49	81	130	8.7	9.0
Heart	75	35	110	123	54	177	3.9	6.0
Kidney	73	27	100	105	33	138	3.0	3.6
Liver	88	43	131	98	39	137	4.7	4.3
Lung	71	30	101	87	33	120	3.3	3.7
Pancreas	73	133	206	116	155	271	14.8	17.2
Spleen	77	26	103	107	38	145	2.9	4.2
Thymus	56	190	246	88	224	312	21.1	24.9
Tongue	69	159	228	94	194	288	17.7	21.5
Tripe	58	60	118	—	—	—	6.6	—
VEAL								
Brain	44	61	105	45	66	111	6.8	7.4
Heart	73	36	109	112	41	153	4.0	4.5
Kidney	65	39	104	112	53	165	4.3	5.9
Liver	81	59	140	92	68	160	6.5	7.6
Lung	71	21	92	80	24	104	2.4	2.6
Pancreas	70	135	205	124	132	256	15.0	14.6
Spleen	79	20	99	102	23	125	2.2	2.6
Thymus (Sweetbreads)	71	27	98	79	26	105	3.0	2.9
Tongue	77	56	133	112	75	187	6.2	8.3
Tripe	54	94	148	—	—	—	10.4	—
PORK								
Brain	49	76	125	52	78	130	8.5	8.7
Chitterlings	42	183	225	—	—	—	20.3	—
Heart	73	42	115	101	43	144	4.7	4.8
Kidney	71	29	100	108	43	151	3.2	4.7
Liver	89	40	129	92	43	135	4.4	4.7
Lung	62	21	83	71	28	99	2.3	3.1
Pancreas (Sweetbreads)	87	98	185	121	98	219	10.9	10.8
Spleen	77	23	100	120	29	149	2.6	3.2
Tongue	71	151	222	103	167	270	16.7	18.6
LAMB								
Brain	47	72	119	54	83	137	8.0	9.2
Heart	74	51	125	93	47	140	5.7	5.2
Kidney	67	29	96	98	31	129	3.2	3.4
Liver	91	67	158	101	98	199	7.4	10.9
Lung	74	23	97	89	27	116	2.6	3.0
Pancreas	63	94	157	99	87	186	10.5	9.6
Spleen	77	25	102	116	34	150	2.8	3.8
Tongue	63	160	223	92	185	277	17.7	20.5
Tripe	65	60	125	—	—	—	6.6	—

*Kizlaitis and others, "Nutrient Content of Variety Meats," *Food Technology.*
Siedler and others, *Nutritional Quality of Variety Meats.*
†All separable fat removed before cooking.

CALORIE AND FAT CONTENT OF 100 GRAMS
OF CURED AND PROCESSED MEATS*†

	Energy (Calories)	Fat (grams)
Bacon	630	65
Bologna	220	16
Braunschweiger	280	24
Corned beef	290	25
Dried beef	200	6
Dutch loaf	190	14
Frankfurter	200	14
Head cheese	240	20
Kolbase	310	29
Liver sausage	260	21
Salami	430	37
Salami, cooked	310	27
Salt pork	780	85
Country style sausage	310	27
Polish sausage	270	23
Pork sausage, fresh	450	45
Smoked sausage link	350	32
Summer sausage	410	35
Thuringer	290	24

*Chatfield and Adams, *Proximate Composition of American Food Materials.*
Schweigert and Payne, *A Summary of the Nutrient Content of Meat.*
†Analyses were on samples as purchased, without further cooking.

8

The Special Extras

There is no question that proper use of herbs, spices, and wine in cooking is of major importance. The cook who uses them to flavor food with a combination of courage, imagination, and restraint, is a cook who can produce interesting and delicious meals.

Herbs and Spices that Complement Meat

There is a world of difference between the wonderful taste of corn, cooked and eaten a few hours after it has been picked, and the tastelessness of corn prepared several days after it has been picked. The difference in taste between fresh and dried herbs is just as dramatic, as is the difference in taste between freshly ground spices and their commercially ground counterparts. It is possible to buy fresh parsley and dill in many parts of the country almost all year; but unfortunately other fresh herbs often are only available in perennially warm climates or in the summer, unless you are willing and able to grow some of them indoors.

Since it is virtually impossible to avoid using dried herbs occasionally, it's useful to know that one *teaspoon* of dried herbs is the equivalent of one *tablespoon* of fresh herbs. It's best to buy both spices and dried herbs in small quantities because they lose strength as they grow older. Keep them in tightly closed containers, in a cool place, away from strong light. Dried herbs can be pepped up by soaking them in a very small amount of liquid, such as olive oil, stock, or water, just before you use them. Some fresh herbs can be frozen, and although they won't be as good as fresh herbs, they will be considerably better than dried.

Allspice Goes well with beef, pork, and sausage. Use to season sauces, stews, soup, and marinades.

Basil Fine with beef, veal, lamb, pork, and liver. Particularly good with any dish that includes tomato. Use to season soup and stews. Cook for a short period of time. Use fresh whenever possible.

Bay Leaf Enhances the flavor of beef, lamb, and liver. Good seasoning for soup, stews, and marinades. Bay leaves are an essential ingredient of a *bouquet garni*. They should be used sparingly and should always be removed before food is served.

Caraway Seed A nice touch in beef, pork, sausage, liver, and kidney dishes. Sometimes also used to season stews.

Cayenne A good seasoning for beef, pork, and sausage. Use to season sauces, stews, and marinades. A small amount goes far.

Celery Leaf A fine flavoring for lamb. Excellent as a seasoning in soup, stews, and marinades.

Celery Seed Goes very well with beef and veal. Use to season sauces, soup, stews, and marinades.

Chervil Excellent with beef, veal, and lamb. A nice seasoning for sauces, soup, and stews. Chervil should be added to food only at the last minute, and should be used fresh whenever possible.

Chili Powder Particularly good with beef. Use to season sauces and marinades, but use sparingly.

Chives Go well with most meat. A good seasoning for sauces, soup, and stews.

Cinnamon An interesting flavor with lamb, beef, pork, tongue, and sausage. Often used in sauces—both sweet and sour.

Cloves Good with beef, lamb, pork, tongue, and smoked sausage. Used to season soup, stews, and marinades. Whole cloves should be removed from soup and stews before serving. Use ground cloves sparingly.

Coriander Seed Very nice with beef, pork, and sausage. A good seasoning for soup and stews.

Curry Powder Excellent with beef and lamb. An unusual seasoning for sauces and stews.

Dill Superb with lamb and beef. An excellent seasoning for sauces and soup. Dill should not be cooked for a long period of time.

Dill Seed Also very good with beef and lamb. Use to season sauces and soup.

Fennel Goes with beef, pork, and sausage. A nice seasoning in sauces and stews too.

Garlic Can be used with most meat, particularly beef and lamb. It is also used to season sauces, soup, stews, and marinades. When garlic is used whole, it should be removed from food before food is served. When garlic is sautéed, be sure to avoid overcooking, which will produce a bitter flavor. Garlic powder is a very poor substitute for fresh garlic which is always available and keeps very well. Use a garlic press or smash a clove of garlic with the flat side of a heavy knife, discard peel, and chop.

Ginger Excellent with beef, pork, and sausage. Use to season sauces and marinades. Fresh ginger can be frozen and then grated without being defrosted. Fresh, frozen, or powdered ginger must be cooked in order for the flavor to be released.

Horseradish If you like the very strong taste of freshly grated horseradish, you will enjoy using it with beef and tongue and as a distinctive addition to many sauces.

Juniper Berries Very good with veal and pork and as a seasoning in marinades.

Marjoram Can be used with beef, veal, pork, lamb, mutton, and sausage. Use as a seasoning in sauces, soup, and stews.

Mint Good with lamb and as a seasoning for some sauces.

Mustard Goes well with all meat and can be used as a seasoning in almost all nonsweet dishes. Dry mustard and good French prepared mustard have a stronger and better flavor than most domestic prepared mustards. Prepared mustard is made from mustard seeds. Seeds are available for use in pickled food.

Nutmeg An interesting flavor with beef, veal, lamb, sausage, and in some sauces. Use freshly ground whenever possible. A nutmeg grater is inexpensive and worth having.

Oregano Particularly good when used in moderation with beef, veal, pork, and kidneys. Fine as a seasoning in sauces, soup, and stews.

Paprika A good seasoning for beef and veal. Use to season stews and as an aid in browning meat. You will find a very real taste difference in Hungarian, Spanish and domestic paprika. Hungarian paprika is very strong and has a distinctive flavor; Spanish paprika is not as strong; and domestic paprika is almost tasteless. All kinds of paprika are excellent for garnishing.

Parsley This most versatile herb can be used with all meat and to season almost everything except desserts. It is an essential ingredient of a *bouquet garni* and a superb garnish. Fresh parsley bears almost no resemblance to dried parsley and fresh sprigs can be stored in the refrigerator for several days. To store properly, wash, shake dry, wrap in paper towels, and place in a plastic bag.

Pepper Complements all meat and can be used to season almost everything except sweet foods. The flavor and aroma of freshly ground pepper is superior to commercially ground pepper. A good pepper mill is a very worthwhile investment.

Rosemary Very good with beef, veal, lamb, pork, and kidneys. Use as a seasoning in soup, stews, and marinades.

Saffron Enhances the flavor of veal and lamb but must be used very sparingly to avoid a medicinal taste. Use saffron threads rather than powdered saffron which is not always genuine. Saffron can also be used as a yellow coloring agent.

Sage Can be used with beef, veal, lamb, pork, and sausage. It is an excellent seasoning for stews and sauces, but it must be used in moderation.

Salt The correct amount of salt to use depends on individual preference and sometimes on diet restrictions. Properly used, salt brings out the natural flavor of all food, including sweets.

Savory Fine with beef, veal, lamb, pork, and sausage. A good seasoning in sauces and soup.

Sorrel Very nice with pork and as a seasoning in soup.

Soy Sauce Particularly good with beef and as a seasoning for sauces and marinades. Soy sauce is salty, therefore the amount of salt used in the same recipe should be adjusted accordingly.

Tarragon Excellent with beef, veal, and sweetbreads. A superb seasoning for sauces and soup.

Thyme Very good with beef, veal, lamb, pork, mutton, and kidneys. Use to season sauces and stews. Thyme is an essential ingredient of a *bouquet garni*.

Note: It is easier to control the amount of salt added to a recipe if you use onion or garlic *powder* instead of onion or garlic *salt*. But neither of them is a satisfactory substitute for the real thing and they should be avoided whenever possible.

Wine and Meat—A Good Marriage

Wine used in cooking should be good enough to drink. If you don't like the taste of a wine when you sip it, you won't like the taste of it in food. The alcohol in wine evaporates at 172.4° F (lower than the boiling point of water), but the flavor is intensified during cooking. Therefore, if a wine is bitter, sour, or too sweet when it is added to a recipe, the unwanted taste will be even stronger by the time the cooked food reaches the table. So-called "cooking wine" and "cooking sherry" have salt added to them. Since their flavor is inferior to the flavor of table wine and sherry, they should be avoided. There is really no need to use them because it is not difficult to buy decent wines at modest prices.

Choosing the correct wine to go with a specific food is not always easy, but there are a few general observations that can be helpful. A strong robust red wine will overpower the light delicate taste of veal and pork. On the other hand, if you are serving a hearty beef stew, the flavor of light white wine will be completely lost. That is why a robust red wine generally is used with red meat and in brown sauces, and a white wine usually accompanies a paler more delicate tasting meat and is used in pale sauces. Fortified wines, such as sherry and Marsala, are used as flavoring in basting, marinades, sauces, and soup. They are not generally used as part of the liquid in which meat is cooked.

Select a dry wine rather than a sweet one for meat dishes. When a recipe calls for a dry white wine, you can safely substitute a dry white vermouth in most cases. You will find it is less expensive than most white wines, and after it has been opened it will keep nicely for a longer period than an unfortified wine.

Recipes for marinades often include wine because it is a superb tenderizer, and it adds a delightful flavor to meat. Since wine is less acid than vinegar and not as potent, it may be necessary to marinate meat slightly longer if wine is substituted for vinegar in a marinade.

Don't be afraid to experiment. Start by substituting a small amount of wine for water in a given recipe. When it is added to the liquid in which meat is cooked, begin with one-quarter to one-half cup of wine per pound of meat. Try one tablespoon of wine per cup of sauce or gravy, until you have determined exactly how much wine flavoring you like. Use wine to deglaze a pan in which meat has been roasted or sautéed. You'll have the basis of a delicious sauce or gravy.

When you serve wine with a meal in which wine has also been used for cooking, be sure to serve either the same wine at the table or one that is compatible. However, if your table wine is exceptionally fine and expensive, it is an unnecessary extravagance to use the same wine in cooking. Much of the subtlety and nuance of the flavor will be overpowered by the food and the seasoning. Choose a less expensive wine instead, one that will go with the more expensive table wine. Don't hesitate to seek the advice and help of a wine merchant. Most knowledgeable dealers will be glad to help you make a good choice. You may also find it very helpful to buy one of the many excellent books available on cooking with wine.

9

Carving

Carving is an ancient art which, for a time, seemed to be in serious danger of becoming a lost one. In medieval times, part of every young nobleman's education was learning how to carve with grace and ease. The process of carving was almost ceremonial and was considered an integral part of the presentation of a meal. During the earlier part of this century carving often was relegated to the kitchen. Meat was simply brought to the table already sliced and, as a result, often not very hot. Happily, carving at the table is gaining popularity once again. Anyone can do it, but it helps to know what you are about.

Proper carving begins with carvable meat. You also need good knives that are finely honed and razor sharp, the proper surface to cut on, and some knowledge of the anatomy of the meat to be carved. Practice helps, too. Artful carving is the result of experience, knowledge, and good equipment. There is an added bonus. Slices of well-carved meat are more tender than pieces that have been hacked off with a dull knife.

Start With Meat That Can Be Carved Easily

Successful carving begins at the meat counter because some cuts of meat are easier to carve than others. You can ask your butcher to bone, or partially bone, many hard-to-carve cuts. A leg of lamb, for example, is quite easy to carve if the sirloin section containing the hip bone is removed before the leg is cooked. You can save the sirloin chops and use them for another meal. A square-cut shoulder also may be hard to carve, but you can have it boned and rolled.

The boneless cuts shown in Chapter 2 are available in most markets. It is increasingly easy to find boneless and semi-boneless smoked hams, boneless smoked shoulder rolls, boneless pork loin roasts, boneless legs and shoulders from both veal and lamb, as well as rib roasts that have had the chine bone (and often the featherbones) removed. More and more boneless cuts from beef chuck and round are also appearing in food stores across the country. If carving properly has been a problem, discuss the cut of meat you want with your butcher next time you plan to serve a roast. If you decide to have him bone a roast for you, don't forget to take the bones home for the stockpot!

Prepare Meat Correctly for the Carver

The way meat is cooked can make a difference in how easy it is to carve. If a roast is cooked at a very high temperature, it may form an outer crust that will make carving extremely difficult. On the other hand, if braised meat is overcooked, the meat will fall apart when it is carved, no matter how sharp the knife is.

As mentioned in the chapter on cooking methods, allowing a roast to "set" after cooking will make it firm enough to carve properly. This is not true, however, for steaks and chops, which should be served immediately after they are removed from the broiler or skillet. It's preferable to have guests wait for a steak, instead of having a steak wait for the guests.

Whenever possible, strings and skewers should be removed in the kitchen. If you are concerned about the possibility that a rolled or stuffed roast may fall apart during carving, leave one or two strings in place. Center the roast on a carving board (wood is preferable), large enough to allow the carver to cut the meat without spilling on the tablecloth, and small enough to avoid having the size of the carving board make the roast look small and insignificant.

Equipment for Carving Meat

Meat cannot be carved properly, in fact it cannot really be carved at all, without proper equipment. An inadequate carving surface and a dull knife are guaranteed to ruin the most beautifully cooked meat.

The most satisfactory carving surface is wood. Meat slides on **Carving Boards** china platters. Metal, including silver, will not only be scratched by a knife, but will also dull the blade. A good carving board should have either a "well" to catch juices, or it should be built on a slight slant, with a lip so the juices will collect at the back of the board and not run off onto the table. Try to avoid using carving boards that have prongs on which to anchor meat. Juice will escape through the holes the prongs make, and you will not have the mobility you need to shift the angle or location of the meat during carving. It's a good idea to have at least two carving boards in different sizes—a large one for big roasts (and for turkey) and a smaller one for small roasts and steak. Good carving boards are quite expensive, but with proper care they should last for many years. After using a wooden board, wash it with a gentle soap in cool water, rinse well, and dry immediately. Never submerge a wooden carving board in water. Excessive moisture will cause it to warp and eventually crack. If grease is difficult to remove, use coarse salt and the remains of half a squeezed lemon.

Whether intended for carving, boning, paring, chopping, or **Knives** general slicing, knives should be well-made (which also means they will be expensive), sharpened regularly, washed properly, and stored correctly. Poorly made knives will not take a sharp enough edge to cut efficiently, and the desperate effort involved in trying to make them perform is both frustrating and time consuming. A cheap knife is a waste of money. A good knife will pay for itself many times over in satisfaction and in its long life.

There is considerable controversy on the subject of carbon steel knives versus stainless steel. Many professional cooks prefer carbon steel because they feel it will take a sharper edge than stainless steel. However, stainless can be sharpened very well if the sharpener is made of a substance harder than the knife. Since it is not possible to determine how hard a metal is by looking at it, it's a good idea to shop in a store that has a knowledgeable salesperson who can give you information and guidance on which knives and sharpeners to buy. Stainless has the added advantage of being rustproof. Some of the newer imported knives are made of an alloy that is harder than any sharpener made. To the extent it is possible to sharpen these knives at all, it is necessary to do so on a china plate which is harder than the alloy.

A well-made knife is perfectly balanced, has a hand-ground blade, a comfortable handle, a deep forged shoulder or finger guard, and usually has rivets that attach the upper end (or tang) of the blade to the handle. The tang should extend well into the handle. Avoid knives that are held together with glue instead of rivets. The newest kind of handle uses neither glue nor rivets, but is made of molded polypropylene that is permanently bonded to the blade.

Hollow-ground blades are made by machine and cannot be sharpened properly, but they function perfectly well if they

The standard carving set includes a knife with a curved blade 8 to 9 inches long, a matching fork, and a steel. This size knife is best suited for carving medium size roasts.

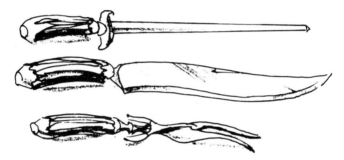

The roast slicer and carver's helper are a good combination, but are seldom sold as a set. They both come in a variety of sizes and shapes and are designed to carve standing rib roasts, whole or half hams, and other large cuts of meat. A good roast slicer should have a long flexible blade, at least 11 inches long, that can cut across a large surface. The carver's helper should have widely spread tines to hold a large roast steady.

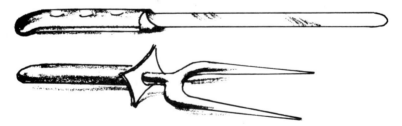

The steak set is a junior edition of the standard carving set. The blade of the knife is usually 6 to 7 inches long and is ideal for cutting steaks and chops.

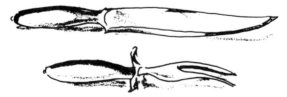

have a serrated edge. Choose knives according to function: small knives for paring; larger knives for chopping, cubing, mincing, and dicing; serrated knives for cutting bread or tomatoes; narrow thin-bladed knives for boning; a cleaver for cutting through bone and for tenderizing; and knives that have the proper length, shape, and degree of rigidity or flexibility for carving different kinds of meat. Three examples of carving knives and their uses are shown in the illustrations on the preceding page.

A knife should never be placed in a dishwasher. The heat of a dishwasher affects the tempering, and soaking is not good for either the blade or the handle. Avoid putting a knife in a sink full of soapy water. It's too easy to reach into a full sink and inadvertently grab a sharp knife by the blade. Wash knives separately in hot soapy water, rinse well, and dry them immediately, then put them away promptly. Don't store knives loose in a drawer, but keep them in a slotted box, or, better still, hang them in a knife rack where they will not be dulled rubbing against each other. The safest racks are also slotted and should be securely attached to a wall out of the reach of young children. If you use a magnetic rack, be sure the magnets are strong enough to hold the knives securely in place and that the knives are clean. A greasy knife will not adhere properly to a magnetic rack.

Knife Sharpeners

To maintain a finely honed edge, a knife should be sharpened every time it is used. If you want to keep your knives in top condition, sharpen them before or after each use just as automatically as you wash them. Electrical and mechanical sharpeners are not nearly as satisfactory as a hand-operated steel. Since each blade is different, it can be dulled or chipped if it is not sharpened by hand. No mechanical or electric sharpener can take into account the individual size or shape of a knife. Furthermore, mechanical and electric sharpeners often shorten the life of a knife by wearing away too much of the blade.

Choose a sharpener made of a substance harder than the blade to be sharpened and made in a shape you find comfortable to use. Be sure there is a guard at the end of the steel to protect your hand. Many of the steels that come with knife sets have a relatively rough grain. If the grain is very rough, you will need a second steel with a fine grain or a fine grain stone to give the edge of your blade a finishing touch. It's a good idea to have your knives sharpened professionally about once a year. The illustrations that follow show the correct way to sharpen a knife.

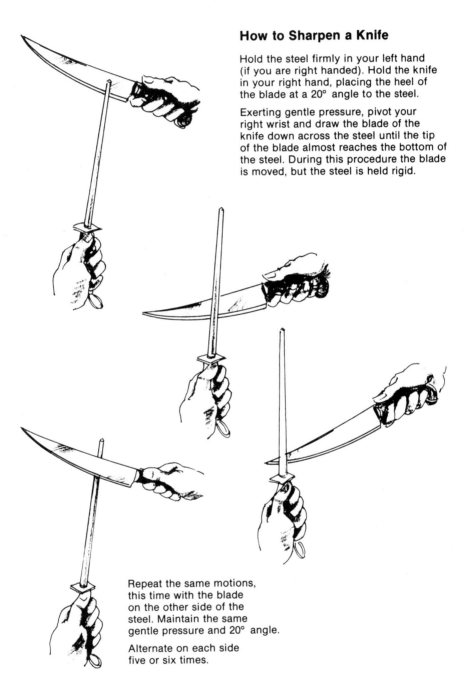

How to Sharpen a Knife

Hold the steel firmly in your left hand (if you are right handed). Hold the knife in your right hand, placing the heel of the blade at a 20° angle to the steel.

Exerting gentle pressure, pivot your right wrist and draw the blade of the knife down across the steel until the tip of the blade almost reaches the bottom of the steel. During this procedure the blade is moved, but the steel is held rigid.

Repeat the same motions, this time with the blade on the other side of the steel. Maintain the same gentle pressure and 20° angle.

Alternate on each side five or six times.

"The Performance"—Time to Carve

Assuming you have before you a reasonably easy-to-carve cut of meat, properly cooked, sitting on the correct size carving board, a well-sharpened knife, and an attentive and hungry audience, then what? Start by making yourself comfortable. Although at one time it was considered a breach of etiquette to stand while carving, it is perfectly acceptable today. Most people find it easier to carve in a standing position, but if you prefer to sit, by all means do so. Move everything out of the way—water and wine glasses, gravy boats, candles, dishes of other food, even garnishes. Warm plates on which to serve the meat should be nearby, but not in the way.

Determine which way the fibers run in the meat and where the bone, if any, is located. Anchor the meat firmly with a sturdy two-pronged carving fork. Try to avoid piercing the meat with the fork too often because juices escape each time a fork is plunged into the meat. Most meat should be sliced *across the grain*. Technically meat is not really made more tender by slicing across the fibers or grain, but the shorter fibers you get by slicing this way make the slices seem more tender. There are exceptions: some comparatively thin cuts of meat, such as flank steaks and corned beef briskets, are sliced diagonally across the grain and very tender cuts such as one-inch loin and rib steaks can be carved with the grain.

Use a gentle sawing motion. Don't change the angle of the knife once you have begun to slice. Make uniform slices and place them neatly to one side on the carving board if there is room, or overlap them "shingle" style on a warm serving platter. It's preferable to carve all the meat you think you will need for the first serving before you serve anyone, so you can divide the slices evenly. You can always return to the carving board to slice more meat when it is time for "seconds." If you anticipate having leftovers, leave some meat unsliced. A solid piece of meat will not dry out in the refrigerator as soon as slices.

The illustrations that follow show the best methods for carving a number of meat cuts.

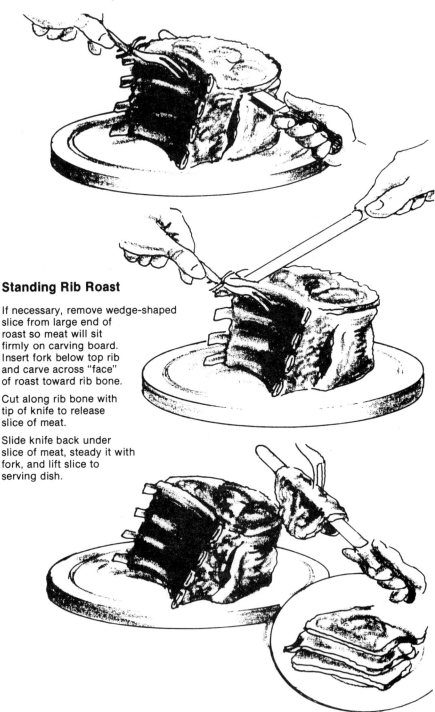

Standing Rib Roast

If necessary, remove wedge-shaped slice from large end of roast so meat will sit firmly on carving board. Insert fork below top rib and carve across "face" of roast toward rib bone.

Cut along rib bone with tip of knife to release slice of meat.

Slide knife back under slice of meat, steady it with fork, and lift slice to serving dish.

Beef Blade Roast

Cut between muscles and around bones to remove solid sections of meat.

Position cut section so meat fibers run parallel to platter.

Carve meat across the grain, making slices about ¼ inch thick.

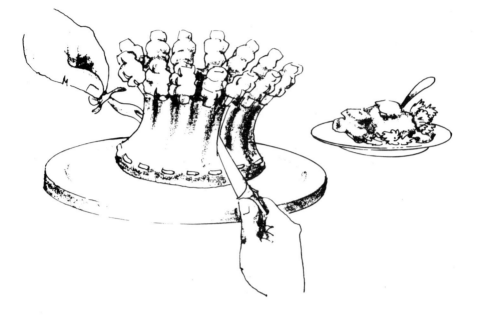

Crown Roast

Remove any garnish from center
of crown roast that may
interfere with carving.

Slice down between ribs,
removing one rib at a time.

Pork Loin Roast

Remove back bone, leaving as little meat
on it as possible, before roast is
brought to the table.

Place roast on
platter, rib side facing
carver. Insert fork in top of roast.
Slice meat by cutting closely along
each side of rib bone. One slice will
contain a rib. The next slice will be boneless.

Rolled Roast

Strings may be removed
before roast is brought to
the table or, if necessary,
may be removed at the table.
Since rolled roasts are
boneless, they are easy
to carve. Hold firmly in
place with fork and slice.

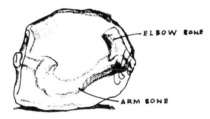

Picnic Arm Shoulder

Cut two or three slices from base and turn roast so it rests on surface just cut.

Cut down to arm bone at point near elbow bone. Turn knife and cut along arm bone to remove boneless arm meat.

Carve boneless arm meat by making perpendicular slices.

Remove meat from each side of arm bone. Slice boneless pieces of meat.

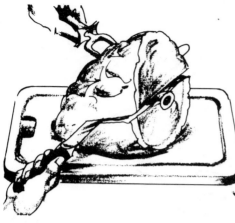

Half of Ham

Place shank end on carver's left with cushion portion of ham on top. Cut along top of bone and lift off cushion portion.

Place cushion portion on carving board and make perpendicular slices.

Cut around leg bone with tip of knife to remove meat from bone. Turn meat so thick side is down and slice.

Place on carving board with "face" down. Cut along bone to remove boneless section. (This section may be on either the right or the left, depending on whether it came from a right leg or a left leg.)

Place boneless section on carving board and carve across the grain.

Hold remaining section with fork and carve across meat toward aitch bone. Release cut slice from bone with tip of knife and lift on to platter.

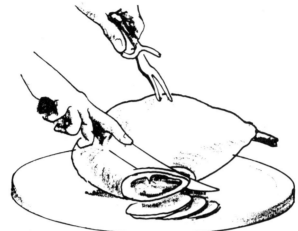

Leg of Lamb

Cut two or three slices of meat from the base of the leg.

Turn roast so it sits on surface just cut. Start slicing where shank joins leg. Make perpendicular slices toward leg bone.

Loosen slices by cutting under them along top of leg bone. Lift off slices and place on serving dish.

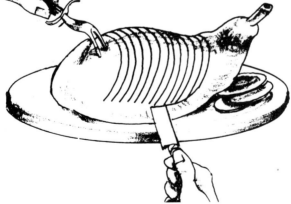

10

The Proper Equipment

Whether you are a talented chef or someone who enters the kitchen only under the compulsion of hunger pangs, you should have proper equipment in the kitchen. Without it, cooking can be difficult, time consuming, and unnecessarily complicated. But with proper equipment—much of which is simple and inexpensive—a great many cooking chores are less complicated, and the results are more accurate and sometimes almost foolproof.

Gadgets are fine for those who can afford them, have room to store them, and enjoy using them. But for cooks who have no particular interest in gadgets, the problem often is how to determine whether a product is a gadget or an important and useful piece of equipment. The answer may lie in the kind of cooking a person does, or in a thorough and clear understanding of how a particular piece of equipment functions. Gadgets aside, some equipment is basic. Much of the equipment discussed on the following pages is essential for everyone who wants to cook meat correctly and with ease.

Equipment Related to the Cooking of Meat

Barbecue Equipment

The kind of equipment you need to cook meat out-of-doors depends entirely on how extensively you are likely to use it. It's possible to build a perfectly good fire in a small portable grill or hibachi. But, if you plan to do a great deal of outdoor cooking and entertaining, a large well-made grill is a worthwhile investment. Buy one that is rust-resistant and has a heavy hood to conserve heat and block wind. Choose a model that can be adjusted easily so you can control the distance between the fire and the grill. A well-made grill will also have closely spaced grids to prevent small pieces of food from falling into the fire. Grid rods should be made of plated nickel or chrome. Some models are designed so you can add additional coals to the fire when necessary, without removing partially cooked food. If you are going to invest a substantial amount of money in a grill, this is a feature worth having. A grill should be designed so it can be taken apart easily for cleaning. Some grills have electric spit motors, which must be properly grounded and should rotate at the rate of six revolutions per minute. If you decide to invest in a gas grill, be sure the burner knobs can be removed or locked in the "off" position.

You'll find outdoor cooking easier and safer if you also invest in asbestos mitts, long-handled utensils, tongs, and a stiff, heavy, metal brush to clean the grill. Add a convenient work space near the grill and you'll be all set to enjoy an outdoor dinner.

Baster A baster is used to suck up liquid (fat, juice, or a glaze) from the bottom of a roasting pan so the liquid can then be released over meat. A spoon can be used to accomplish the same thing, but it is much easier and far more efficient to use a baster. Simple basters can be purchased for a dollar or less; fancy ones cost slightly more. They are not efficient tools for skimming fat (see Skimmers); but they are indispensable for keeping hands and fingers from being burned (which is what can happen when a spoon is used for basting).

Carving Boards See Chapter 9 on carving.

Cheesecloth Cheesecloth is invaluable, inexpensive, and sometimes difficult to find. For some strange reason, it seems to have almost vanished from the shelves of many supermarkets.

With determination, however, you probably will be able to find it in a drugstore or hardware store. Use it to wrap herbs for a *bouquet garni*, to wrap food to be poached, to wrap around a cut lemon that is to be squeezed, and as a superb fine-strainer for stock and other liquids.

Chopping and Cutting Boards

A good chopping or cutting board is indispensable in the preparation of food. A Formica counter may seem adequate as a cutting surface, but it's not suitable because the surface can be damaged and, since Formica is not resilient, knives are often damaged as well. The best chopping surfaces are made of the end grain of wood. A large, rectangular piece of heavy butcher block is an excellent cutting surface because it is resilient. Be sure to wash butcher block, or any wood surface on which meat is cut, carefully and thoroughly to prevent the growth of bacteria on the surface. This is very important because wood is porous and grease is difficult to remove. If, for sanitary reasons, you are concerned about using wood, it is possible to substitute hard rubber, hard plastic, or ceramic. Hard rubber stands up very well, but plastic will scratch and chip and eventually have to be replaced. Ceramic will also scratch and, since it has no resilience, it will be uncomfortable to use and may damage your knives. Whatever material you choose, be sure to get a board that is heavy and will not slide around as you chop.

Cooktops

There are three major kinds of cooking surfaces available today: gas burners, standard electric burners, and smooth ceramic electric cooktops. They are available both as part of a range or as a separate unit. Many people have no choice between gas and electric, either because they must use equipment already installed in an apartment or house, or because they live in a house without a gas line or which does not have adequate electric wiring. If you replace a cooktop, and have adequate wiring, you do have a choice between the familiar standard electric burners or the new smooth ceramic cooktops.

There are advantages and disadvantages to ceramic units. They are easy to keep clean, attractive to look at, maintain good steady temperatures, and can double as extra work space. However, they heat more slowly than conventional burners and they can be seriously damaged if the wrong cleansers are used. Moreover, in order for them to work effectively, the pots and pans used on them must have completely flat bottoms. Although one manufacturer provides a few new pots with the cooktop, purchasing a ceramic unit usually means you must buy new pots and pans as well. In recognition of this problem, one model is made with one burner that will accommodate any kind of pot. But a cook who has a favorite set of pots and pans, and who may already have a substantial investment in good cookware, may prefer to have gas or standard electric burners.

All cooktops should be vented. A relatively new cooking unit, vented down instead of up through an overhead fan, is now available. This type of unit can be a major advantage if you want to place a cooktop in the center of a kitchen, provided you have no objection to the fact that the vent must occupy a small amount of precious counter space. This unit is convertible and can be used as an indoor barbecue, a griddle, a rotisserie, a deep-fryer, or with standard or ceramic electric burners—and they are all interchangeable!

There are important factors to keep in mind in selecting a cooktop. It should have steady controls that go accurately from very low to high heat, good ventilation, and an overhead light. The cooktop should be easy to clean and safely located in a convenient spot in the kitchen. Heat-resistant counter space, to accommodate hot pots and pans, should be adjacent to the cooktop.

Garlic Press If you like the flavor of garlic with meat, and if you use garlic often, you'll find a well-made garlic press worth having. Choose one that is easy to clean.

Graters A great many foods used in the preparation of meat dishes require grating. Cheese, ginger, fresh horseradish, nutmeg, nuts, parsley, vegetables, and zest (citrus peel) are but a few. Graters come in many sizes and shapes. Some are electric and some are hand-operated. Most are difficult to clean. You probably will find that several different kinds of graters are more convenient than one all-purpose grater. Cheese, nutmeg, and parsley graters are all worth having and they are not expensive.

Grinders Whether you have an old-fashioned hand-operated meat grinder, a sleek, modern electric grinder, one of the miraculous new labor-saving food processors that grind meat, or a grinder attachment for a multi-purpose appliance, you should have something in your kitchen for grinding meat. Investing in a good meat grinder, even a relatively expensive one, will save money in the long run. You'll be able to grind leftovers to use in imaginative casseroles and croquettes. You can grind economical cuts of meat for hamburgers. An added advantage to grinding your own meat is that it provides an opportunity for you to control the amount of fat added. Once you've tasted a hamburger made from freshly ground beef, you'll never want to be without your own grinder.

Heat Regulator

A heat regulator is precisely the kind of equipment that some people consider an unnecessary gadget and others find indispensable. A round metal object for either electric or gas burners, it sits on top of a burner and provides a layer of hot air, which is more gentle under a pot than direct heat. It's an enormous improvement over an asbestos pad and, in many instances, can take the place of a double boiler. The layer of air makes possible the safe use of a relatively fragile casserole or pot on top of a burner. In addition, it provides a steady, gentle heat. Therefore, scorching and burning are virtually eliminated. It has the added advantage of being inexpensive.

Knives

See Chapter 9 on carving.

Larding Needles

It would be startling indeed to find a well-equipped French kitchen that doesn't have a larding needle. It's almost as startling to find an American kitchen that does. Earlier chapters explained that the more marbling (flecks of fat) meat has, the more tender it is, and usually the more expensive it is. Less tender (and therefore less expensive) roasts, and meat such as veal, do not have natural marbling. They can be made tender by the insertion of narrow strips of fat throughout the meat. This process is called larding and it's accomplished with a larding needle. Meat that must normally be cooked by moist heat to make it tender can be larded and then cooked by the dry heat method, an inexpensive way to have a tender oven roast. Larding needles can be bought for as little as a dollar or for as much as twenty dollars. The investment will pay for itself many times over in money saved by buying less expensive cuts of meat to roast.

Ovens

Modern technology has provided vast improvements in standard gas and electric ovens and has also provided entirely new kinds of ovens. In addition to the familiar gas and electric units, microwave and convection ovens are now available for home use. Innovations in standard ovens provide self-cleaning features, timers that can turn the oven on and off automatically, built-in meat thermometers, and rotisseries. Self-cleaning models do use extra energy during the cleaning process; but they are enormous time savers and eliminate the cost of expensive oven cleaners. In addition, self-cleaning ovens are particularly well-insulated in order to self-clean safely. The extra insulation reduces the amount of energy required for cooking.

To be reliable, an oven should be level and the inside temperature must be accurate at all times. Use an oven thermometer to check the temperature inside your oven and to determine if it maintains a steady accurate temperature. If it doesn't, call a serviceman and have it calibrated. As a matter of fact, you probably will find that any time a serviceman is on hand to fix your oven he will be willing to check the temperature and make an adjustment if necessary. Calibrating an oven is usually a quick and simple procedure for which there probably will not be an extra charge.

Microwave ovens differ widely from model to model, but the principles on which they operate are the same. The advantage of a microwave oven is the speed with which it cooks. Microwaves provide a type of electro-magnetic energy that food absorbs but which does not heat the air that surrounds the food. The waves pass through paper and glass and some kinds of plastic and ceramic, but not through metal, which is why metal pans cannot ever be used. All types of microwave ovens offered for sale must pass stringent tests at the laboratories of the Bureau of Radiological Health, a division of the United States Department of Health, Education, and Welfare, that certifies their safety.

A microwave oven should not be thought of as a replacement for a standard oven, but rather as a companion to it. It has both advantages and disadvantages. To begin with, a microwave oven is not inexpensive and, except for people who frequently must cook meals quickly, it can hardly be considered a necessity—although it is a very convenient piece of equipment. It is excellent for defrosting food (which certainly is handy if you forget to take dinner out of the freezer or have unexpected company), heating leftovers rapidly without having them dry out, and reducing the time required to cook food.

The time needed for cooking will vary according to the particular model and the amount of food placed in the oven. The cooking time may also be affected by the temperature of the food when it is placed in the oven. Less tender cuts of meat that require slow cooking by moist heat will not be as tender if they are cooked in a microwave oven. Finally, meat cannot be broiled in a microwave oven.

Convection ovens have been used commercially for many years but models designed for home use are fairly new. Cooking time in a convection oven is longer than in a microwave oven but shorter than in a conventional oven. A fan in the convection oven continuously circulates heated air, removing the cold air around the food and replacing it with moving heated air. As a result, food is heated more evenly than in a conventional oven, cooking time is reduced, and food is cooked at a lower temperature. The combination of using a lower temperature and a shorter cooking period also means considerable savings in energy. All food that normally can be cooked in a standard oven can be cooked in a convection oven, although cooking times and temperatures must be adjusted. While only two or three companies have residential models available at the present time, it is likely that more models will become available in the near future as the advantages of convection oven cooking become more widely known.

Pastry Brush

This useful kitchen tool is poorly named. It has many more uses than just painting an egg glaze on pastry. A well-made pastry brush, which will not lose bristles, is not expensive. It is an invaluable aid in spreading barbecue sauce and other sauces on the surface of meat. Its use provides good control so you can cover meat with a nap (a thin layer), or with a heavy coating. A pastry brush is also a useful tool for greasing utensils. And of course if you make a meat pie with a crust, you'll need a pastry brush to glaze the top of your pie.

Pepper Mill

When pepper is used it should be freshly ground. Compare the taste of foods seasoned with commercially ground pepper and with freshly ground pepper. Then rush out and buy at least two pepper mills—one for the kitchen and one for the table.

Pots and Pans So much can be said about pots and pans that entire books have been written on the subject. Not only is there an endless assortment of sizes and shapes, but there is also a wide variety of different materials used to make them. The most important thing to keep in mind is that you get exactly what you pay for. A really heavy well-made utensil will be expensive, but it will last almost indefinitely. Even more important, it will cook food properly. A cheap pot will not only need to be replaced in a short period of time, but it may burn and scorch food and cook it unevenly. It is much better to have a few really good pots and pans than a cabinet filled with badly made ones. A pot should be heavy and well balanced, with a secure sturdy handle and a tight-fitting cover. Although thick, heavy copper pots, lined with tin or silver, are undoubtedly the best and the most expensive pots you can buy, even they are not suitable for cooking every kind of food. And upkeep on good copper pots can be expensive, since they must be periodically re-tinned. Cast iron pots are also excellent, but they are difficult to take care of because they rust easily. Heavy gauge aluminum is a fine heat conductor, and aluminum pots work well, provided certain foods like wine, vinegar, lemon juice, and egg yolks are not cooked in them. The best kind of aluminum pots are heavy and are lined with stainless steel. Stainless steel by itself is not a very good conductor of heat. An all-stainless pot may be quite durable, however, and its long life could turn out to be a disadvantage, if it doesn't cook food properly. Heavy pots lined with enamel are excellent—until the enamel chips. Use them carefully and they'll serve you well.

A well-equipped kitchen should have two or three frying pans in different sizes, several saucepans with tight fitting lids, a heavy dutch oven, a small and a large roasting pan, a large stock pot, and a few covered casseroles in a variety of sizes.

Pressure Cookers There are both advantages and disadvantages to using a pressure cooker. Cooking time is cut appreciably, reducing food preparation time and providing a substantial saving in the amount of energy used. However, many meat dishes that require long, slow cooking are enhanced by the melding of flavors that takes place during cooking. When a pressure cooker is used, and cooking time is reduced, there may be some loss of flavor. That possible loss must be balanced against the saving of both time and use of energy.

Roasting pegs or pins are gadgets, and somewhat ill-conceived ones, at that. A metal roasting peg inserted in a roast conducts heat to the center of the meat. The object of this questionable procedure is to cook meat quickly. The difficulty is that precious juices escape around the peg, the center of the meat gets done too quickly, and the meat is likely to be less tender.

Roasting Pegs

Very few roasting pans come with racks. Those that do have a flat rack that does little more than keep a roast from sitting directly in the drippings at the bottom of the pan. One of the most inexpensive and useful pieces of cooking equipment is an adjustable, V-shaped rack that holds a roast properly and allows hot air to circulate entirely around the surface of the meat. That is the correct way to cook a roast. With this rack you can easily convert almost any shallow pan into an excellent roasting pan.

Roasting Rack

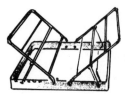

A good kitchen scale is one way to reassure yourself that you have a reliable and dependable meat market. A scale will also come in handy if, when you take a piece of meat out of the freezer, you discover you have forgotten to mark the weight on it. (Frozen meat weighs exactly the same as fresh!) If you buy ground beef in quantity, you'll find a scale helpful in weighing meal-size amounts for freezing. You'll even find a scale useful for dividing ground meat into even patties. When you buy a scale, choose one with both standard and metric weights, so you will still be able to use it when we convert to the metric system.

Scales

There is simply no efficient way to remove excess fat from many dishes unless you have a fat skimmer. If you want to remove fat from a liquid that you don't have to use immediately (like stock), you can chill it. This will cause the fat to rise to the surface, where it solidifies and can be lifted off easily with a knife. But if you are ready to serve a stew that has too much fat in the liquid, you'll need a skimmer because a spoon or a baster will remove some of the liquid you want along with the excess fat you don't want. In addition, skimmers are very practical for removing deep-fried food from the fat in which it has been cooked, or for removing a dumpling from the liquid in which it has been cooked. A skimmer is an inexpensive, useful, multi-purpose tool. If you don't already own one, treat yourself to one next time you go shopping. You'll be surprised at how many ways you will use it.

Skimmers

Slow Cookers   The principle of cooking food slowly at a low heat for a long period of time is not new, but the emergence on the market of an imposing, and often confusing, array of electric slow cookers is fairly recent. A slow cooker can be the perfect solution for someone who is away from home all day and who would like to come home to a piping hot dinner, cooked and ready to eat. Even those who are home during the day will find a slow cooker useful. This is a pot that does not need watching, although it may be necessary to experiment when you first use it to avoid overcooking food. Slow cookers use a minimal amount of energy and provide a fine method for cooking less tender cuts of meat.

Choose a slow cooker with heat coils on the bottom and around the sides, rather than only on the bottom. This will insure even cooking. Some pots also have removable coils for easy clean-up. Check to be absolutely certain the slow cooker you choose will bring the temperature of the food to 125° F within three hours and then rise quickly to 165° F. These temperatures are necessary to destroy bacteria growth. It's wise, the first time you use a slow cooker, to test the temperature of the food with a food thermometer. If the temperature does not rise high enough within the specified time, return the cooker and select one that will meet this vital safety standard.

Tenderizers   Certain cuts of meat are pounded to make them tender and
(Mallets and   very thin. Pounding breaks down tough fibers and improves
Cleavers)   texture. It can be done with the flat side of a cleaver or, more easily, with a mallet. A metal mallet does a good job. Inexpensive mallets are usually made of wood, but unfortunately wooden mallets are not very good because they generally are not heavy enough to do a good job. They also are difficult to clean. If you have no particular use for a heavy meat cleaver and you don't want to invest in a good metal mallet, you'll have to depend on a meat cutter to do your pounding for you.

Thermometers   A well-run kitchen is equipped with several thermometers. They are not gadgets. They are vital and necessary tools that tell you if food is being stored at safe temperatures, if your oven is cooking at the correct temperature, if meat is ready to serve, if oil is hot enough to cook with, and if your sauce is being maintained at the proper temperature. Obviously, if a thermometer is not accurate it is useless. If it is difficult to read, it is almost useless. Choose thermometers that are clearly marked and well made.

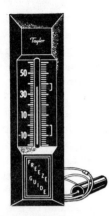

Remote Reading
Freezer-Refrigerator

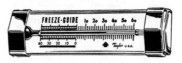

Refrigerator-Freezer

Glass Tube
Meat

Oven

Deep Frying

Roast and Yeast

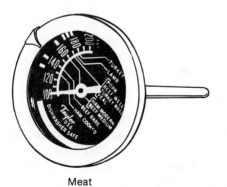

Meat

Microwave Oven
"Instant Reading"

It has been customary for many years to insert a meat thermometer in a roast for the entire time the meat is cooking. However, when a meat thermometer is used this way, it creates the same difficulties as a roasting peg. Juices escape and the center of the meat gets done too quickly. It's better to cook a roast by the clock and test it with a thermometer shortly before you think it's done.

Professional cooks often use a "Bi-Therm Dial Thermometer" that comes in a convenient case with a pocket clip. They are able to carry it with them and whip it out to test a roast or any food they want to check. This marvelous little thermometer registers the temperature of the food almost instantly. Although it is more expensive than other food thermometers, it's a worthwhile investment, and it can be used to test any food within a range of 0° F to 220° F.

Food thermometers function best if they are warmed or cooled under running water before they are inserted into very hot or cold food.

Tongs Every time you stick a fork into meat you make holes in it through which juices escape. It's much better to turn meat with a pair of tongs. (If you are adept at using chop sticks, you can use them instead of tongs to turn small pieces of meat.)

Research Equipment Before You Buy

Money spent for well-made cooking equipment is money well spent. But before you decide what to buy, take time to research what is available. An afternoon spent window shopping in appliance stores, department stores, specialty shops, and even hardware stores can pay off. You'll get a good overview of what is available, how well it is made, and what it costs. Ask your friends and acquaintances, particularly those who enjoy cooking, to tell you what equipment they find most helpful. And ask them to tell you why. One source of information and specific evaluation of cooking equipment is *The Cooks' Catalogue* (Harper & Row, 1975). This book is well-organized and carefully researched and can serve as an invaluable guide for good cooking equipment.

11

Away From Home

Menus are not always written in English. But it's fun to be able to order with confidence when the waiter arrives, even though the menu contains little or no English. You may be surprised to discover how easy it is to become familiar with foreign food terms, even though you don't speak a particular language. There is an added advantage, too. Although an ethnic cookbook may be written in English, its recipe titles often are not. It helps to know exactly what kind of food a recipe is for when you read a table of contents or check an index.

Here is a list of foreign words and terms that relate to meat and meat dishes which should be helpful the next time you find yourself face to face with an intimidating menu.

ENGLISH	FRENCH	GERMAN	ITALIAN	SPANISH
appetizer	hors d'oeuvres	Vorspeise	antipasto	Entremeses variados
bacon	lard de poctrine fumé	Speck	pancetta	tocino
baked	cuit au four	gebacken	al forno	al horno
beef	boeuf	Rindfleisch	manzo	vacca
beefsteak	bifteck	Beefsteak or Bifteck	bistecca	biftec
boiled	bouilli	gekocht	bollito	hervido
bone	os	Knochen	osso	hueso
brains	cervelle	Hirn	cervella	sesos
breast	sein	Brust	petto	pecho
broiled	grillé	geschmoren	alla griglia	asarse
broth	bouillon	Kraftbrühe	brodo	caldo
butter	beurre	Butter	burro	mantequilla

ENGLISH	FRENCH	GERMAN	ITALIAN	SPANISH
calf	veau	Kalb	vitello	ternero
cheese	fromage	Käse	formaggio	queso
choice	de choix	excellent	scelto	selecto
chop	côte; côtelette	Kotelett	costoletta	chuleta
chopped	haché	gehackt	tritato	picado
cold	froid	kalt	freddo	frío
(to) cook	faire cuire	kochen	cucinare	cocinar
cooked	cuit	gekocht	cotto	cocinado
cream	crème	Sahne	crema	crema
crust	croûte	Kruste	crosta	corteza
cut	morceau	Schnitt	taglio	corte
cutlet	escalope	Kotelett	cotoletta	chuleta

dish	mets	Gericht	piatto	manjar
dry	sec	trocken	secco	seco

eggs	oeufs	Eier	uova	huevo

fat	graisse	Fett	grasso	grasa
filet or fillet	filet	Filet	filetto	filete
flour	farine	Mehl	farina	harina
fresh	frais	frisch	fresco	fresco
fried	frit	gerösten or gebraten	fritto	frito

garlic	ail	Knoblauch	aglio	ajo
gravy	sauce or jus	Sosse	sugo	salsa
grilled	grillé	gegrillt	ai ferri	a la parrilla

half	demi	halb	mezzo	medio
ham	jambon	Schinken	prosciutto	jamón
hamburger	viande hachée	Frikadelle	am burghese	hamburguesa
hash	hachis	Gehacktes	carne trita	picadillo
heart	coeur	Herz	cuore	corazón
heavy	lourd	schwer	pesante	pesado
homemade	de la maison	hausgemacht	alla casalinga	casero
horseradish	raifort	Meerrettich	ravanello	rábano picante
hot	chaud	heiss	caldo	caliente

kidneys	rognons	Nieren	rognoni	riñones

lamb	agneau	Lammfleisch	agnello	cordero
lean	maigre	mager	magro	magro
leg	gigot; gigue	Keule	coscia	pierna
lemon	citron	Zitrone	limone	limón
liver	foie	Leber	fegato	hígado
local	du pays	örtlich	locale	del país

ENGLISH	FRENCH	GERMAN	ITALIAN	SPANISH
meat	viande	Fleisch	carne	carne
meatball	boulette	Fleischklöschen	polpetta	albondiga
medium	à point	gar	a punto	a medio asar
milk	lait	Milch	latte	leche
mixed	mélangé	gemischt	misto	mixto
mushrooms	champignons	Pilze	funghi	hongo
mustard	moutarde	Senf	senape or mostarda	mostaza
mutton	mouton	Hammelfleisch	montone	carnero
nut	fruit sec; noix (walnut)	Nuss	noce	nuez
oil	huile	Öl	olio	aceite
olive oil	huile d'olive	Olivenöl	olio d'oliva	aceite de oliva
onion	oignon	Zwiebel	cipolla	cebolla
paprika	paprika	Pfefferschoten	paprica	pimenton
parsley	persil	Petersilie	prezzemolo	perejil
pepper	poivre	Pfeffer	pepe	pimienta
pie	tarte	Pastete	torta	pastel
plain	simple	einfach	semplice	sencillo
poached	poché	verlorene	in camicia	escalfar
pork	porc	Schweinefleisch	maiale or carne di porco	cerdo
potato	pomme de terre	Kartoffel	patata	patata
rare	saignant	halbroh	poco cotto	poco asado
raw	cru	roh	crudo	crudo
red wine	vin rouge	Rotwein	vino rosso	vino tinto
rib	côte	Rippe	costola	costilla
rice	riz	Reis	riso	arroz
roasted	rôti	gebraten	arrosto	asado
roast beef	rosbif	Rinderbraten	rosbif	rosbif
salad	salade	Salat	insalata	ensalada
salt	sel	Salz	sale	sal
sandwich	sandwich	belegtes Brot	panino imbottito	emparedado
sauce	sauce	Sosse	salsa	salsa
sausage	saucisse	Wurst	salsiccia	salchicha
shoulder	épaule	Schulter	spalla	espalda
sirloin	faux-filet	Lendenstuck	lombo	solomillo
slice	tranche	Schnitte	fetta	rebanada
smoked	fumé	geräuchert	affumicato	ahumado
soup	potage	Suppe	zuppa	sopa
sour	aigre	sauer	agro	agrio
spaghetti	spaghetti	Spaghetti	spaghetti	macarrones
spicy	piquant	scharf	piccante	picante
steak	entrecôte or bifteck	Rumsteack	bistecca	lonja

ENGLISH	FRENCH	GERMAN	ITALIAN	SPANISH
stew	ragoût	Ragout	stufato	guisado
stuffed	farci	gefullt	farcito	relleno
sweet	doux or sucré	süss	dolce	dulce
sweetbreads	ris de veau	Bröschen	animelle	lechecillas
tenderloin	filet	Filet	filetto	filete
thick	épais	dick	spesso	espeso
thin	mince	dünn	sottile	delgado
tomato	tomate	Tomate	pomodoro	tomate
tongue	langue	Zunge	lingua	lengua
veal	veau	Kalbfleisch	vitello	ternera
vegetable	légume	Gemüse	vegetale, verdure, or legume	legumbre
vinegar	vinaigre	Essig	aceto	vinagre
well-done	bien cuit	durchgebraten	ben cotto	bien asado
white	blanc	weiss	bianco	blanco
whole	entier	ganz	intero	entero
wine	vin	Wein	vino	vino
young	jeune	jung	giovane	joven

French Menu Terms

Assiette anglaise: Assorted cold cuts or cold meat

Blanquette d'agneau: Lamb stew with vegetables, garnished with mushrooms and onions, served in cream sauce

Blanquette de veau: Classic veal stew, with mushrooms and onions, in cream sauce

Boeuf à la mode: Beef stew with vegetables

Boeuf Bourguignon: Braised beef cooked in red wine with onions and mushrooms

Carbonnade à la flamande:	Slices of beef, browned, and cooked in beer
Châteaubriand:	Thick broiled steak cut from the heart of the tenderloin of beef
Coeur de filet:	The heart of the tenderloin of beef (the Porterhouse steak section)
Entrecôte:	Rib steak
Escalopes:	Thin slices of meat
Filet de boeuf rôti:	Roast fillet of beef
Fondue Bourguignonne:	Cubes of choice beef, cooked on individual skewers briefly in hot oil, served with a variety of sauces
Médaillon:	A small round cut of meat
Petite Marmite:	Rich meat soup with vegetables
Plat du jour:	Specialty of the day
Pot-au-feu:	Boiled beef dinner with vegetables
Steak au poivre:	Steak cooked with crushed peppercorns
Tournedos:	Small thick fillets
Vol-au-vent:	Large puff pastry shell which can be filled with meat, seafood, or chicken

French Menu Terms
(continued)

German Menu Terms

Bremer Küchenragout:	Meat and vegetables combined in a rich cream sauce
Doppeltes Beefsteak:	Châteaubriand
Faschierter Braten:	Meat loaf
Fleischbrühe:	Meat broth
Holsteiner Schnitzel:	Veal cutlet topped with a fried egg and anchovy
Junges Lamm:	Baby lamb
Kalbsbraten:	Roast veal
Kalbsschnitzel:	Thin veal cutlet
Königsberger Klopse:	Meatballs in savory sauce
Lendenschnitten:	Fillet of beef
Ochsenmaulsalat:	Cold meat salad
Pastete:	Puff pastry shell filled with meat
Pfefferpotthast:	Well-spiced meat and onion casserole
Pichelsteiner:	Meat and vegetable casserole
Sauerbraten:	Marinated braised beef
Schnitzel:	Thin slices of meat, usually veal
Schweinerippchen:	Spareribs
Wienerschnitzel:	Breaded veal cutlets

Abbacchio:	Baby lamb
Bistecca alla fiorentina:	Broiled or grilled steak, seasoned with oil and lemon
(alla) Bolognese:	Cooked in tomato and cheese sauce
Braciole:	Thin slices of beef, usually rolled and filled
Bue allo spiedo:	Beef cooked on skewers
(alla) Cacciatora:	Cooked in tomato sauce
Coratella:	Lamb and variety meat stew
Filetto alla mignon:	Fillet of beef
Involto di carne:	Stuffed and rolled meat
Lasagne alla genovese:	Casserole of broad noodles, meat, cheese, and tomato sauce
Manzo stufato:	Beef stew
Ossobuco:	Veal shank braised in tomato sauce
Piatto del giorno:	Specialty of the day
Prosciutto:	Ham, thin-sliced
Saltimbocca:	Veal cooked with ham
Spaghetti con carne:	Spaghetti with meat sauce
Spezzatino di vitello:	Veal stew
Tritato misto:	Mixed grill
Vitello tonnato:	Veal served with tuna fish sauce

Italian Menu Terms

Spanish Menu Terms

Ajiaca:	Meat and potato stew
Biftec:	Steak
Caldo gallego:	Thick meat and vegetable stew
Carbonada:	South American meat stew
Cocido español:	Thick beef or chicken and vegetable soup
Cordero en ragout:	Lamb stew
Enchilada:	A kind of Mexican tortilla stuffed with meat
Filetes empanados:	Veal fillets, egg-dipped and fried
Fabada asturiana:	Pork and beans
Guisado español:	Beef stew made with olive oil and onions
Olla podrida:	Vegetable and meat stew
Pecho de ternera:	Breast of veal
Pierna de cordero:	Leg of lamb
Puchero:	Stew
Salsa española:	Spanish sauce
Tamale:	A thin fried cake made of cornmeal and filled with meat
Tortas de carne:	Meat patties
Tortilla:	Omelet, often combined with various kinds of meat. In Mexico a thin flat cornmeal cake

Glossary

In order to follow a recipe correctly, whether it is simple or complicated, you should understand the special language of food and cooking, which occasionally sounds strange and mysterious. The list that follows cover the terminology used in buying and cooking meat and meat dishes.

Acidulated Water Water to which one tablespoon of vinegar or lemon juice is added per quart of water. Used primarily in the cooking of variety meats.

Aged Meat Meat treated by controlled temperature and humidity to increase tenderness and flavor, primarily ribs and loin of high-quality beef and lamb.

Animal Fat Fat that comes directly from an animal or is made from an animal product (butter, suet, or lard).

Arm (Cut) One of the seven basic retail cuts, also called shoulder. Comes from the lower section of the chuck in beef.

Aspic A flavored gelatin which can be made with gelatin and meat juices. The liquid in which meat has been cooked may also be used with the gelatin.

Baby Beef (Calf) Meat from cattle three to nine months old, usually weighing between 350 pounds and 550 pounds, which have been fed on milk and grass. Baby beef comes from cattle which are older than veal and younger than beef cattle.

Bake To cook by dry heat in an oven. The process of baking meat uncovered is called roasting.

Barbecue To roast or broil on a rack, grill, or revolving spit. Meat is often basted with a highly seasoned sauce. This term is also applied to food cooked with, or served in, a barbecue sauce.

Bard To wrap pork fat, bacon, or suet around the surface of lean meat before roasting to make meat juicier and more flavorful.

Baron A very large cut of meat. In the United States, baron usually refers to both hindquarters (legs and loins) of lamb. However, in England, where the term originated, baron refers to a roast made from both sirloin sections of beef. In France, baron is the saddle and two legs of mutton and lamb.

Baste To moisten food with a liquid, pan drippings, butter, or sauce during cooking to prevent food from drying out and to add flavor.

Beat To mix or stir liquids or solid foods thoroughly and rapidly by a hand or electric mixer in order to blend them or make them lighter.

Beurre Manié A floured butter ball usually made of equal parts of softened butter and flour; sometimes made of two parts of butter and three parts of flour. Used to thicken sauces and gravies.

Bind To make different foods, or particles of food, adhere to one another, usually through the use of beaten egg, milk, water, or flour.

Binder An ingredient used to hold several foods together or to thicken a mixture.

Blade (Cut) One of the seven basic retail cuts, also called shoulder. Comes from the upper portion of the chuck in beef.

Blanch To reduce strong flavors in meat such as bacon, ham, or salt pork by plunging them into boiling water and cooking for a specified time. Also done to soften or wilt food other than meat, and to facilitate the removal of skin from certain foods.

Blend To combine foods by stirring, rather than beating.

Boil To cook in liquid at a temperature of 212° F. Bubbles will rise to the surface and break.

Boil Down To boil liquid until it is decreased by evaporation. To reduce.

Bone To remove bones.

Boned or Boneless A cut of meat from which the bone has been removed.

Bottom Round Large muscle found in the outside portion of the round.

Bouillon Stock or broth made by simmering meat and other ingredients in liquid, which is then strained and clarified. Available commercially in concentrated form at food markets.

Bouquet Garni Small bundles of herbs and spices wrapped in cheesecloth or tied together and added, for flavoring, to liquid in which food is cooked. Herb bundle must be removed before a sauce or gravy is made and before food is served.

Braise To cook meat at a low temperature with a small amount of liquid in a tightly covered pan, either on top of the range or in the oven.

Brand Name The same as "Packer Brand Name." Refers to a grade or quality of meat determined by a packer or processor, rather than by the United States Department of Agriculture.

Bread To coat food with bread crumbs, cracker meal, cornmeal, or flour, usually using beaten egg or milk to help coating adhere to food.

Breast (Cut) One of the seven basic retail cuts. Includes the brisket and short plate in beef, the breast in veal and lamb, and spareribs and bacon in pork.

Brine Heavily salted water, used in the preservation of food.

Broil To cook by direct heat in a broiler, or to grill over hot coals.

Broth A clear soup, often made from stock.

Brown To darken the surface of meat by direct heat or in a pan.

Butt The sirloin portion of a full beef loin that has been separated from the short loin. Also the upper end of a ham, now more correctly termed rump.

Butterfly To split food (such as a chop or cutlet) in half, leaving halves hinged on one side. When spread open, food resembles a butterfly.

Canner Lowest USDA grade designation for beef. Not sold at retail. Used primarily in canned meat, sausage, and ground meat.

Carcass The dressed (cleaned), slaughtered animal that contains both "sides"—two forequarters and two hindquarters.

Carve To slice cooked meat with a sharp knife.

Casing Outside covering of sausage which is made from either natural animal intestines, other natural products, or man-made materials.

Casserole A combination of two or more foods, baked and usually served in a dish that is also called a casserole.

Center Slice An oval shaped slice of ham containing a small round bone and cut from an area approximately one inch on either side of the center cut. The center cut divides the ham into rump and shank halves.

Chill To make food cold without freezing it.

Choice USDA grade designation below Prime for beef, veal, and lamb.

Chop To cut food into small pieces. Also, a cut of meat.

Chuck Slightly more than one-quarter of the total carcass of beef. Located in the front section, it contains the first five ribs and includes blade roasts, arm pot-roasts, cross rib pot-roasts, and meat appropriate for grinding and making stew.

Clarified Butter Melted butter from which the milky residue has been removed. Butter is heated over gentle heat and, as the butter melts, a white deposit collects on the bottom of the pan. The clear fat is clarified butter which, when heated, will not burn as easily as butter that has not been clarified.

Clarify To strain fat or solids from a liquid in order to make it clear. Stock is sometimes clarified by straining and by the addition of egg whites that attract the cloudy particles in stock, and which then may be removed by additional straining.

Clod A common name for a lean, boneless, large, outside muscle located in the chuck.

Closed Side Right side of a beef carcass.

Coat To cover food lightly, but thoroughly, with a dry or liquid substance.

Combine To mix ingredients together.

Commercial One of the lower USDA grade designations for beef. Usually sold as ground meat.

Condiment A sauce, relish, or spice eaten with food or used to season food.

Conformation The form or shape of a carcass. One of several factors used to determine the grade of veal, pork, and lamb.

Consommé A clear, seasoned stock or broth, often used in the making of soup, gravy, or sauce.

Cool To allow food to stand until it is no longer warm to the touch.

Corned Meat that has been cured in brine.

Correct Seasoning   To taste food during cooking, or just before serving, and add additional seasoning if necessary. Occasionally to reduce a strong flavor by liquid or an equalizing substance.

Cracklings   Crisp pieces of cooked pork rind from which fat has been rendered.

Cream   To mix a softened solid like butter with a solid ingredient like flour, sugar, or crushed garlic.

Croquette   A combination of minced foods shaped in a ball, dipped in crumbs or batter, usually deep-fried and served with a sauce.

Cube   To cut food into small square chunks.

Cubed Steak   Boneless piece of meat that has been mechanically tenderized by machine or by pounding with a mallet.

Cull   Lowest USDA grade designation for veal and lamb.

Cure   To preserve food by drying or other processes, often through the use of salt or a salt solution.

Cutability   A percentage measurement of the quantity of usable meat that can be realized from a carcass.

Cutter   The second lowest USDA grade designation for beef. Used primarily in canned meat, sausage, and ground meat.

Dash   Less than one-eighth teaspoon.

Deep-Fry   To cook food by immersing it in hot fat.

Deglaze   See page 122.

Degrease   To remove excess accumulated fat or grease from a liquid or a cooking utensil.

Demi-glace   A sauce, usually brown, which has been thickened and reduced and is used as a base for other sauces.

Devil   To season food with spicy ingredients such as hot mustard, red peppers, or chilies.

Dice   To cut food into very small uniform cubes.

Dilute   To make a substance thinner by adding liquid to it; to reduce either the strength or flavor of a liquid.

Dissolve   To melt fat over low heat or to make a solution by adding liquid to a solid substance.

Dot   To place small pieces of butter or other food substance over the surface of a food.

Drain To remove liquid that surrounds a solid substance, like meat.

Dredge To coat food with flour or other dry substance.

Drippings Juices and melted fat that remain in the pan after meat has been cooked by dry heat.

Dumpling Dough or stiff batter, dropped into soup or spooned over a casserole before cooking.

Dust To sprinkle surface of food or cooking utensil lightly with a dry substance, such as flour or sugar.

Enrichment Adding food such as egg yolk, cream, or butter to a sauce, often at the last minute.

Establishment Number A number given to a meat packing or processing plant when it complies with all requirements for federal inspection. It appears on the inspection stamp and identifies the plant.

Extract A concentrated essence of a food. Meat extract can be made by reducing meat stock (usually beef) to a thick paste.

Fabricated Cuts Cuts of meat, from wholesale or primal cuts, with some or all of the bone removed.

Fell A thin, tough membrane that covers a lamb carcass.

Filet (Fillet) A boneless strip of meat. Also to cut into boneless slices or to bone.

Filet Mignon A beef tenderloin steak.

Flambé To pour warm liquor, such as brandy, over food, ignite it, and allow it to burn briefly.

Flank The section on both sides of a carcass that lies next to the short plate and beneath the loin.

Flour To cover food or a cooking utensil with a thin layer of flour.

Fold To blend a light mixture such as beaten egg white, with a heavier mixture such as a sauce base, without decreasing the volume of the lighter mixture.

Fondue (Beef) Small cubes of tender beef, usually fillet, speared on a long slender fork, cooked briefly in hot oil, and served with a variety of sauces. Served in the same way as cheese fondue or chocolate fondue.

Force-meat A combination of puréed meat and seasonings, used as stuffing. It may also be shaped, cooked, and served as a first course, or used as an ingredient in a variety of French recipes.

Forequarter Either half of the front section of a side of beef. Includes ribs one to twelve, chuck or shoulder section, brisket, shank, and plate.

Foresaddle Unsplit forequarter of veal, lamb, or mutton.

Freeze To subject food to a very low temperature, causing liquid in food to solidify. Correct freezer storage is 0° F or below.

Freezer Burn Discoloration of frozen meat due to loss of moisture and oxidation. Caused by improper wrapping.

Fricassee Meat that has been cut into small pieces, sautéed in butter, floured, and then simmered in liquid so it produces its own thickened sauce.

Frill A paper ornament slipped over rib or leg bones to decorate meat, particularly crown roasts of lamb and pork, lamb chops, and legs of lamb.

Frizzle To fry food until crisp and curled.

Fry To cook food in hot fat—deepfry, panfry (sauté), and stir-fry.

Garnish To decorate food with attractive foodstuffs, such as parsley or lemon wedges. Also a food used as a decoration on other food.

Glaze To brush or spoon an aspic, sauce, or sugar mixture over food for added flavor and eye appeal. To reduce meat stock to a thick paste for use as a coating for meat or in sauces and gravies. Also a coating brushed on food.

Good USDA grade designation below Choice for beef, veal, and lamb.

Grade USDA or brand name that indicates quality or yield of meat.

Grease To rub fat onto the surface of a cooking utensil.

Grill To cook food over hot coals or under a broiler. Also to broil.

Grind To cut food into very small pieces in a meat grinder or food mill.

Ham Cured and smoked meat from the hind leg of pork.

Hanging Weight The weight of a carcass or portion of a carcass before any fat and bone have been trimmed off.

Hash To chop or cut food into small pieces.

Hindquarter Either half of the back section of a side of beef. Includes the round, loin, flank, and kidney.

Hindsaddle Unsplit hindquarter of veal, lamb, or mutton.

Hip   See Sirloin (Cut).

Hotel Rack   Unsplit rib portion from foresaddle of veal, lamb, or mutton.

Interlard   See Lard.

Julienne   To cut food into long, thin, match-like strips.

Kabobs   Small cubes of meat cooked on a skewer.

Kosher   Description of meat, that has been slaughtered, inspected, and processed according to Jewish law.

Lard   Rendered and clarified pork fat. Also to insert thin strips or lardoons of salt pork, pork fat, or bacon into meat, such as veal, which lacks adequate natural marbling. A larding needle is used to insert the fat. Larded meat is usually cooked by dry heat.

Lardoon   Narrow strips of fat such as pork fat, bacon, or suet. Used in larding.

Leg (Cut)   One of the seven basic retail cuts. This hind portion of a carcass is called the round in beef, leg in veal and lamb, and fresh ham in pork.

Loin (Cut)   One of the seven basic retail cuts. Located between the rib and the sirloin or hip.

Marbling   Flecks of fat that can be seen in meat. The presence of marbling and the amount of it in a cut of meat adds to the tenderness and flavor of meat and is a major factor in determining quality grade of beef.

Marinade   An acidulated liquid (vinegar, wine, or citrus juice), combined with seasonings and sometimes with cooking oil, in which meat is allowed to stand before cooking. A marinade enriches flavor and usually tenderizes meat. It is often used to baste meat during cooking.

Marinate   To let food stand in a seasoned liquid (marinade), in order to add flavor to it and often to tenderize it.

Marrow   A fatty edible substance found in the center of bones.

Mask   To cover food completely with an aspic or a sauce; to make a flavor indistinct.

Mince   To cut or chop food into very fine pieces.

Monosodium Glutamate (MSG)   A white, crystalline substance that has no taste of its own but brings out the flavor of other foods.

Mutton   When sheep reach their first birthday their meat is no longer considered lamb. It becomes mutton.

Nap To cover food with a sauce thick enough to coat it and at the same time thin enough so it will not obscure the outline of the food.

Open Side Left side of a beef carcass. Also called "loose side."

Panbroil To cook meat slowly, over moderate heat, uncovered in a skillet, removing all fat as it accumulates.

Panfry To cook meat uncovered in a skillet in a small amount of hot fat. Also sauté.

Parboil To boil food in a liquid until partially cooked, prior to cooking by another method (see Blanch).

Pasties Small meat pies.

Pickle To preserve and flavor food in a brine or a special solution usually made of spices and vinegar.

Pinch Less than one-eighth teaspoon or literally, the amount of seasoning that can be picked up between the thumb and forefinger.

Planked Meat that is cooked and served on a seasoned board, usually surrounded by other cooked foods.

Plate A combination of the short plate and the brisket.

Poach To cook food covered by a liquid at a temperature just below simmering.

Portion Control Cut Steaks and chops which have been cut to specified weights and thicknesses.

Potted A canned, seasoned meat mixture.

Precook To cook food either partially or completely, before using the food to complete a recipe.

Preheat To heat an oven, broiler, or skillet to a desired temperature prior to placing the food in it.

Preserve To prepare food for use at a later time through specific methods such as curing, smoking, or canning.

Pretendered A process by which meat is made tender through the use of harmless enzymes or mechanical means.

Primal Cut See Wholesale Cut.

Prime Highest USDA grade designation for beef, veal, and lamb. This is the best grade for special aging and is the grade most often served in the finer restaurants.

Rasher A portion, usually two or three slices, of bacon.

Reduce To decrease the volume of a liquid by boiling it rapidly, (see Boil Down).

Render To change fat from solid to liquid by heating. Rendered fat can be used for cooking and its use will add special extra flavor.

Rib (Cut) One of the seven basic retail cuts. Located between the shoulder and the loin.

Rind The outer skin of some foods. Usually removed before food is eaten.

Roast To cook food by dry heat, uncovered, usually in an oven, occasionally over hot coals.

Rolled Roast A rib roast that has been boned and tied.

Round Slightly less than one quarter of the total of a beef carcass. Located in the hind section, back of the loin.

Roux A mixture of flour and fat, usually in equal proportions, cooked together, and stirred constantly, to form a smooth paste. Used as a thickening or binding agent for sauces and gravies.

Rump A section of round that lies next to the loin in beef and is a portion of a whole ham.

Saddle A large cut of veal, lamb, or mutton. See Foresaddle and Hindsaddle.

Sauté To cook food in a skillet or sauté pan in a small amount of hot fat.

Scald To heat a liquid to a temperature just below the boiling point. Also to immerse food briefly in boiling water as in blanching.

Scallop To bake food in layers, usually with cream or a sauce.

Score To make shallow cuts in the surface of meat, usually in a specific pattern.

Sear To brown the surface to meat quickly with intense heat.

Season To add salt, herbs, spices, or other condiments to food in order to enhance flavor.

Short Plate A portion of the forequarter immediately below the primal rib.

Shoulder See Chuck.

Shred To shave or cut food into long narrow pieces.

Side Either half of a beef or hog carcass.

Simmer To cook food in a liquid at a temperature just below boiling point (approximately 185° F). Bubbles form slowly and break beneath the surface.

Sirloin (Cut) One of the seven basic retail cuts. Part of the loin, also called hip.

Skewer To run a long, narrow, sharp-pointed metal or wood pin (called a skewer) through the center of a large piece of meat or through several pieces of meat and other food so they can be cooked together. Also to use a small, slender, metal object to keep an opening in meat closed to contain stuffing.

Skim To remove a substance, usually fat, from the surface of a liquid.

Sliver To cut into long thin narrow pieces.

Smoking A technique used to cure certain cuts of meat by exposing them to smoke from special kinds of wood.

Smother To cover food completely with another food or with a sauce.

Spit To cook food on a large skewer (a spit), over coals or in an oven.

Sprinkle To scatter minute amounts of a dry substance or drops of a liquid over the surface of food.

Standard USDA grade designation below Good for beef and veal.

Steam To cook food by means of the vapor from boiling liquid which rises through the food.

Stir To move a utensil through food with a circular motion in order to mix, dissolve, agitate, or keep food from burning.

Stirfry To cook small pieces of food in a small amount of hot fat over intense heat, usually in a wok. Food is stirred constantly during cooking and is cooked for a very brief time.

Stock A strained liquid in which meat bones, meat, vegetables, and seasoning have been simmered for several hours. Stock is used as a basis for many soups, sauces, and gravies.

Strain To remove solid matter from a liquid by pouring both into a sieve or cloth to separate them.

Stud To press a food substance such as cloves into the surface of a large piece of meat.

Stuff To fill a cavity in food with a different food.

Stuffing A seasoned mixture of food used to fill a cavity in meat, or around which a thin slice of meat may be rolled.

Subprimal Cut A portion of a primal cut.

Suet Hard, crumbly, white fat found around the kidneys and loins of beef and mutton.

Tenderize To make meat tender by pounding, cubing, or cooking in moist heat; or by the use of a substance such as a marinade or tenderizer.

Tenderizer A substance used to soften the connective tissue of meat.

Tenderloin The most tender muscle of the carcass, located inside the loin and running nearly the entire length of the loin.

Thicken To make a liquid substance more dense by adding foods such as flour, egg yolk, cornstarch, or arrowroot, or by additional cooking to evaporate some of the liquid.

Thickening Agent One of the ingredients listed above, used to make a sauce or gravy more dense.

Top Round Inside portion of round.

Toss To flip food over by shaking a skillet or pan or by jerking a covered casserole in a circular up and down motion.

Utility One of the lowest USDA grade designations for meat.

USDA United States Department of Agriculture.

Variety Meats Edible organs and glands of a meat animal. Includes: brains, heart, hog intestines (chitterlings), kidney, liver, spleen (melt), stomach walls (tripe), testicles (fries), thymus (sweetbreads), and tongue.

Whip To beat a food substance, usually a liquid, so air is incorporated into it and it becomes lighter and increases in volume.

Wholesale Cut Also called Primal Cut. A division of the hindquarter or forequarter of beef, a division of the foresaddle and hindsaddle of lamb, one of six divisions of pork, and one of seven divisions of veal. (It may be purchased by consumers who can have it divided into smaller retail cuts. The price per pound of a wholesale cut is usually lower than the price per pound for retail cuts from the same section.)

Yield Grade A numerical grading, from one (the highest grade) to five, that indicates how much usable meat a carcass will provide. These grades are designed to identify cutability differences in carcasses, or the yield of boneless, closely trimmed retail cuts from the round, rib, loin, and chuck.

Metric Measurements and Equivalents

Someday, when the United States joins the rest of the world in using metric measurements, much of the confusion that exists in our present system of measurements will be cleared up. President Ford signed an act in 1975 that encourages the use of metrics, and it seems likely that by 1990 we will pretty well have converted to the metric system. Working with units of ten in our everyday calculations will be much simpler than trying to figure out the sometimes bewildering relationships of pounds and ounces and feet and inches that we use today.

The basic units of the most common metric measurements are **Liters** (for volume), **Grams** (for mass or weight), and **Meters** (for distance). Temperature is measured on the **Celsius** scale, rather than the Fahrenheit.

Prefixes are used to designate the most commonly used quantities of the basic units. **Milli-** describes one-thousandth of the basic unit. **Centi-** is one-hundredth; **Deci-** is one-tenth of the basic unit. **Kilo-** means a thousand times the basic unit. You may run into **"deka-"** (ten times the base unit) and **"hecto-"** (100 times the base unit) from time to time, but they're less frequent than the **"milli-," "centi-," "deci-,"** and **"kilo-"** prefixes.

In dry weights and linear measurements, the terminology of the metric system has universal acceptability. But with liquid measurements, especially when applied to cooking, the tendency is to follow the custom of the leading French cooks, who use large fractions of a liter rather than "milliliters." Standard French and other European cookbooks deal with measurements of one liter, a half liter, a quarter liter, and one-tenth of a liter (which is sometimes written as 1 deciliter). These fractions are fairly easy for us to work with, since we are used to cups and liquid pints and ounces.

Volume Measurements

Our common measurements of cups and spoons, and quarts, pints and ounces, can be quite conveniently expressed in their metric equivalents, at least approximately. These approximations, in liquid measurements, are not scientifically accurate but they are generally close enough to be used in home cooking. Many utensils now available have both metric volume and standard measurements shown on them. This makes conversion easier, and will enable you to continue to use your favorite recipes even when everything else has been changed over to metrics.

Customary Terms (spoons and cups)	Customary Equivalents (ounces, pints, quarts)	Approximate Metric Equivalents
4⅓ cups	1 quart 2 ounces	1 liter
4 cups	1 quart	0.95 liter (1 liter less 1 deciliter)
2 cups + 2½ Tb	17 ounces	½ liter
2 cups	16 ounces (1 pint)	0.475 liter ½ liter less 1½ Tb
1 cup + 1¼ Tb	8½ ounces	¼ liter
1 cup	8 ounces	0.236 liter ¼ liter less ¾ Tb
⅓ cup + 1 Tb	3½ ounces	1 deciliter or ⅒ liter 100 milliliters
⅓ cup (5⅓ Tb)	2⅔ ounces	0.08 liter
3⅓ Tb	1¾ ounces	½ deciliter 50 milliliters
1 Tb (3 tsp)	½ ounce	15 grams 15 milliliters
2 tsp	⅓ ounce	10 grams 10 milliliters
1 tsp	⅙ ounce	5 grams 5 milliliters

Weight Measurements

The basic metric unit for measuring mass (weight) is the gram. A kilogram (a thousand grams) weighs about 2.2 pounds. A pound weighs almost 454 grams, so each ounce is a bit more than 28 grams. The approximate equivalents shown below are usually close enough to work with in the kitchen, but the more precise measurements are included for your convenience if you need them.

Customary Term	Approximate Metric Equivalent	Precise Metric Equivalent
1 ounce	30 grams	28.35 grams
4 ounces (¼ pound)	115 grams	113.4 grams
8 ounces (½ pound)	225 grams	226.8 grams
12 ounces (¾ pound)	340 grams	340.2 grams
16 ounces (1 pound)	450 grams	453.6 grams

Metric Term	Approximate Customary Equivalent
1 gram	¹⁄₂₈ ounce
5 grams	⅙ ounce
10 grams	⅓ ounce
25 grams	a scant ounce
50 grams	1¾ ounces
100 grams	a little over 3½ ounces
250 grams	about 9 ounces
500 grams	1.1 pounds (about 1 pound 2 ounces)
1000 grams	2.2 pounds

The metric standard of temperature measure is CELSIUS (C). Water freezes at 0° C and boils at 100° C, compared with Fahrenheit, where water freezes at 32° F and boils at 212° F. By simple mathematics you can convert to and from either system by using the following formulas:

Degrees Fahrenheit, minus 32, times ⅝ equals degrees Celsius.

$$°F - 32 \text{ times } \tfrac{5}{9} = °C$$

Degrees Celsius, times ⁹⁄₅, plus 32 equals degrees Fahrenheit.

$$°C \text{ times } \tfrac{9}{5} + 32 = °F$$

Here are some relative equivalents that may help establish the relationship for you:

Fahrenheit	Celsius	Description
–10° F	–23.3° C	**Correct freezer temperature**
0° F	–17.7° C	**Highest safe freezer temperature**
32° F	0° C	**Water freezes**
40° F	3.3° C	**Correct refrigerator temperature**
140° F	60° C	**Hot water from tap**
212° F	100° C	**Water boils (sea level)**
250° F	121° C	**Very slow oven**
300° F	149° C	**Slow oven**
350° F	177° C	**Moderate oven**
400° F	204.4° C	**Hot oven**
450° F	232.2° 0	**Very hot oven**

Common pan sizes will be measured in centimeters, instead of inches, when the metric system takes over. One inch equals 2.54 centimeters, and there are 39.37 inches in a meter (something more than a yard). The basic unit is the meter, and like the gram and liter, it is used with the common prefixes to specify smaller or larger length measurements.

A few of the more common pan sizes and their equivalent measurements are:

Customary Measurement	Metric Equivalent
9″ × 9″ × 2″	22 cm × 22 cm × 5 cm
8″ × 8″ × 2″	20 cm × 20 cm × 5 cm
9″ × 5″ × 3″	22 cm × 20 cm × 7.5 cm
8″ round	20 cm round
9″ round	23 cm round
10″ round	25 cm round

Index